CW00551393

Perfect Your
Float Fishing

•PERFECT YOUR•
FLOAT
FISHING

John Bailey

The Crowood Press

First published in 1993 by
The Crowood Press Ltd
Ramsbury, Marlborough
Wiltshire SN8 2HR

British Cataloguing in Publication Data
A catalogue record for this book is available from the British Library.

ISBN I 85223 724 4

Throughout this book the pronouns he, his and him have been used to
refer to both men and women.

Acknowledgements
I would dearly like to thank Peter Drennan, Garry Barclay, Kim Milson,
Ron Lees and Frank Muryeth for all their help in the preparation of this
book.

Picture Credits
Line-drawings by Paul Groombridge.

Picture previous page: the author looks suitably pleased with a lovely float-
caught mirror carp.
Picture on page 6: the float is the perfect tool for the close-in carper,
whatever the conditions.

Designed by
D & N Publishing
DTP & Editorial Services
The Old Surgery
Crowle Road
Lambourn
Berkshire RG16 7NR

Phototypeset by FIDO Imagesetting,
Witney, Oxon
Printed and bound in Great Britain by
BPCC Hazell Books Ltd
Member of BPCC Ltd

Contents

Introduction

Like every other boy, I learned my fishing with the float. In the 1950s ledgering was looked on as something particularly crude and the sort of method a man would only resort to at the very end of an unsuccessful day. In short, you weren't a true fisherman until you had mastered the float. Floats then were gaudy things – bright reds, greens and yellows which appealed to any youngster. They were made almost invariably from quills of some sort with occasional additions of cork, and undoubtedly my happiest memories of childhood are of watching a particular favourite red-tip float of mine bobbing against a variety of backgrounds. That float was a particularly adept perch catcher. The sleeve of cork around it did not appear to inhibit them in any way, whereas the canal roach used to bite far more gently and frequently I would be hovering for seconds, wondering whether or not to strike.

Very sadly, that float came to grief in the most dramatic of ways. I had been 'adopted' by two adult members of the fishing club, and as a mighty treat they offered to take me tench fishing one dawn at a local mill dam. Even now, thirty-odd years on, I can feel the excitement of that morning. It was July, warm and sultry with very little light from sunrise piercing the low cloud cover. There was not a ripple on the dark pool when we arrived, only those from my chopped-up lobworms as I rained them in around the red float.

The low light did not suit my little float. The red did not glow, but looked black against the slightly lighter water surface. Nothing happened for a while, though I was used to that: in the season just gone, I had landed a mere thirty fish in nearly 120 days' fishing! What was that? The float began travelling to my left, and very quickly. It rose from the water and was then gone. Gone! The line parted like a pistol shot. I sat there speechless and Ron, like protector and guide, came running down the bank to me. He checked the line – OK. He pulled at the reel – there was the problem. The clutch was screwed down as tight as it could go on to the spool and nothing would have budged it an inch. A boy whose average catch was a 1oz gudgeon needed to know little about a slipping clutch!

However, the days of the supremacy of the float were already passing. The new breed of specimen hunters, given voice and direction by Richard Walker, were dispensing with floats and leads and simply using hooks at the end of the line, unhampered by any sophistications. Moreover, more big fish were being caught than ever before. Walker's record carp in 1952 was a testimony to the power of floatless tackle, and by the mid-1960s it was not done to be seen with a float on the line – not, that is, if you were to be taken seriously at all. Actually, this was not Walker's fault for he himself continued to use the float; it was we

INTRODUCTION

The float at sunset.

young disciples who took from him what we wanted and discarded the rest. Floats were old-fashioned and redundant, useful only for kids, old men and tiddlers!

By the 1970s, things had changed little. Indeed, one of my own friends once jokingly commented that I didn't even own a float! He was not actually correct, but it was quite possible to see his mistake. By then the specimen hunting method had seriously arrived, and that invariably meant baits hard on the bottom and bite indication at the butt. There was, however, some sympathy for the float man. I think, to some extent, that John Wilson started all this: he wrote a few articles about float fishing for roach using a centre-pin so that float fishing could then be seen as an engaging diversion and an eccentric or elitist method. When I caught my first 6lb tench on the float I and my friends dismissed this as something of a fluke, and the float continued to be the tool of the artist rather than the weapon of the serious fisherman.

By the 1980s, however, all this had changed. I began to fish the River Severn for barbel and it was there that I met Ron Lees. All I could think of was the lead and the swimfeeder and I caught next to nothing. Beside me, Ron would be using the stick float and casters and inching his bait through with delicate perfection. Every barbel that came out during those days fell to Ron, and I began to learn a lesson.

The same thing began to happen back home in Norfolk when some chub, for years suckers for the anchored bait, began to demand something different. In fact, bait had to be moving if it was to be taken at all, and I was forced to relearn the skills and the satisfactions of long-trotting.

On some stillwaters too, carp fishing began to provide some questions. Some heavily fished lakes were bombarded by bolt-rigs and tightly clipped up lines, seasoned through. For the fish it was like running a gauntlet of cheese-wires and they began to sulk badly. Again, a float-fished bait was something new to them and fish began to come out once more.

Now, in the 1990s we have reached a sane balance. Every good angler knows that there are times when to fish lead or a swim-feeder is imperative, but he does not close his mind to the float and the many advantages it can bring. And, of course, float technology has now advanced a million miles. It is hard to buy a quill float today and those I own I have generally made myself. No, modern floats are high-tech and leave the creations of the 1950s lumbering in their wake. Now float fishing is more than an art, it is also a science. To float fish successfully today you need to know which float to use when, where and how. Once again, float fishing is at the centre of our sport, and for efficiency and satisfaction the method simply cannot be beaten.

The roaching master – John Wilson trots the Wensum with a centre-pin.

1 Talking Floats

Why the float? Well, there are times when it will catch dramatically more fish than the lead. Take chub fishing for example. The normal specialist way of going about things is to creep along the river bank, feed in a few pieces of large bait, ledger a worm, slug, piece of flake, lump of meat or cheese and extract two or three fish from the swim before moving on. These might be the largest fish in the area or they might not be. What is definite is that this method only scrapes the surface and only catches a tiny percentage of the chub that are present.

Take an alternative approach: the angler feeds heavily with maggots, hemp, casters or sweetcorn – small baits that really get the entire chub shoal going. The fish begin to forage actively for food, rise off the surface and even take particles as they land. Then the angler puts out a particle under a light, well-shotted, well-balanced float. The presentation is exact and the chub are in a feeding frenzy. By now there is no wariness left in them at all and the float simply buries. And continues to do so again and again. On certain rivers and at certain times it is possible to take forty chub from a swim, not four. That can be the effect of the float – not simply to increase catches but to multiply them tenfold. And, of course, it is likely that more big fish will be caught this way, for the swim is virtually emptied. Everything that is in there will come out to this approach. Of course, I have simplified all this and there are many times when such an approach would not work, but equally there are lots of times when it does and the man who simply sits waiting for his quivertip to go round is missing out on quite sensational sport.

There is little doubt that many anglers do not understand floats at all. Many – no, all – of the top matchmen do of course, and the river 'greats' of history mastered floats better than their own handshake. Just to watch some of the Wessex masters like Gerry Swanton or the late Owen Wentworth trot a float was quite a magnificent, exhilarating sporting event in itself. These men had, or have, lifetimes of experience and can simply make floats talk.

Experience is a very important word here. Let's look at the concept of mending the line. Mending the line is, of course, straightening the line on a river so that it does not form a belly and pull the float off its true course. To some extent the same is true in stillwaters, for if the line does not sink and there is a drift, the float will inevitably be pulled out of its proper resting place. Now, most of us have to mend the line when we are float fishing the river, but the late matchman Billy Lane – who revolutionized fishing in his day – used to criticize mending the line quite soundly. He said that every time the line was mended the float was disturbed, the bait was pulled up and off course, and any big, wary fish got the message. Of course, he was quite right and mending the line can make the float and therefore the bait behave unnaturally – a dead give-away to a coming fish. But, and this is a big but, Billy Lane had float fished all his life and through experience – that word again – he somehow could control a float instinctively without having to mend the line at all. This was greatness born out of years on the river bank and it served him well enough to win him more matches than most of us have had fish.

You also need experience to know how to feather the line perfectly when you're casting a waggler some distance. Feathering involves simply applying a little finger pressure to the spool so that the rate of line exit is slowed down. When done properly, the float simply slows, hangs and enters the exact spot with the minimum splash imaginable. This again takes experience, and the temptation is to feather too strongly or too lightly so that the float lands short in a heap or disappears over the horizon.

You don't, however, need experience to come to terms with some of the float basics; all you need is thought. When the light dawns, float fishing and float comprehension can be quite fascinating.

Consider the shape of a float. If you look at different floats certain things will probably become clear. For example, regard a pear-shaped float. This type of shape casts very well indeed – the heavy bottom shoots it out rather like a dart and it really whistles through the air. However, its stability, especially in running water, is less impressive. In running water, a carrot-shaped float wins hands down. Those bulky shoulders really hold the current and stop the float from wobbling in turbulent water. If you look at the diagram of a typical Avon float, on page 61 (Fig. 20), you will understand how the water film actually rests on the shoulders of the float and almost glues it in position. This helps greatly when the line is being mended, for the float does not come out of the surface film easily and the bait remains virtually unmoved. Were the float shaped with the bulge at the bottom it would rock at the slightest hint of pressure.

Look now at some of the weighted floats. It is common to see the weight built into the bottom end of the float. This is not totally inefficient, but the whole structure does wobble in flight and it is difficult to target the cast exactly. If, however, the weight is put outside the float or at least at the extreme end, then the flight during the cast is absolutely true. As you can see, float design is quite a complex subject but it is one that makes sense with just a little thought.

Materials used in floats also need to be discussed. The old floats made of crow, porcupine and peacock quills were absolutely great. Not long ago, floats were also made out of all sorts of woods and back in Victorian times they were even made of porcelain! These types of materials obviously worked, and they also had a great deal of character and 'soul' about them. One of the attractions was that every float was that little bit different. They weren't mass produced and every single one had to be tested by the angler, the shotting being refined to suit it. Each float would have a different buoyancy, a different flight pattern and sit rather differently in the water. In short, each float behaved completely differently.

Today, however, all that has changed. The individuality of floats has gone now that blow-moulded plastics are with us. It is now possible to know exactly how a given float will behave because it is just one of millions that came from the same mould – quite unlike the multifarious creations of nature. If you lose one float you can put on its exact twin and fish it properly at the very first cast. Although you do lose the soul of the float, what you gain in time and precision is incalculable – very

A lovely chub – the river behind is perfect for the stick float.

important considerations for the matchman in particular, where every second counts.

The new materials also tend to be tougher. Take, for example, the older-style Avon float with its balsa body. You need a tight rubber at the top of the float to grip it firmly or else it is always moving up and down in fast water and on hard striking. The trouble is, by being gripped tightly the balsa is actually penetrated by the line. A groove is worn through the paint and the water gradually seeps in. After a few hours, you often begin to find the balsa Avon sinking lower and lower in the water until it is useless and has to be replaced. The blow-moulded version is impervious to this.

Enormous thought goes into float design today. Peter Drennan makes some of the very best modern floats available on the market – he should do though, for he has years of experience and started making floats over thirty years ago when he was a teenager. He once told me how he used to go into his workshop at the end of the day's fishing to design the exact float for a particular job, a particular swim, and almost a particular fish – perhaps one he had been trying to catch that day! As a result, he built floats that were truly personal, designed perfectly for the most intricate of jobs. He gave me as an example the float that he designed for a particular swim on

Capt L. A. Parker – the roaching maestro with two big fish caught on the centre-pin.

the Royalty. This was in the days of heavy maggot baiting. Being a lad, Peter could not afford the amount of maggots that most other anglers used, but he did notice that many of these men did not feed the maggots in properly. They failed to appreciate the depth and speed of flow in their swim, and very often most of the maggots were swept away downstream into oblivion – or rather into the mouths of a waiting shoal of barbel.

Peter appreciated all this and would walk the banks hoping to find a very profligate, inefficient angler. Once he found somebody piling in maggots, most of which were swept away, he would settle himself downstream and begin to fish where the maggots actually landed. There was one particular spot which always seemed to attract one of the maggot duffers. Fifty yards beneath, the water hurled round a bridge support where a raft of rubbish invariably built up. The maggots would go trundling down towards this raft where they would stick, and where the barbel would feed unheeded.

The trouble was that it was a difficult swim to fish, so everybody avoided it – apart from Peter who built the exact float for the job. It was a huge seabird quill, shaped like a banana with two large corks on it. The shape was perfect for clinging right to the raft and riding the fast current serenely. It allowed the maggots on Peter's hook to be dragged right under the rubbish to where the barbel were feeding avidly on the maggots which were trundling downriver. Only a float could have presented the maggots in exactly the right way . . . and you can imagine the rest!

Modern materials allow you to build your own float in a similar type of way without expertise or a workshop. In fact, the floats are almost Lego-like, and you can swap bits from one to the other to make the perfect float for the job. For example, you can put in a very slim insert tip that shows up shy bites, or you

can take out one coloured top and put in a different coloured top if the light changes. When darkness begins to fall you don't have to change a thing: you simply take out the coloured top and put in a Betalight or a Night Light. If the drift builds up during the course of the day as the wind rises, all you have to do is insert a longer body piece to give the float more stability. Equally, if you want to slow a waggler down, simply lengthen it and the trot through will take far longer. In fact, with the minimum of time and fuss you can adapt the float you set out with at dawn so that you always have on your line the exact tool for the job right through until the following nightfall.

Float fishing demands skill and thought, and this is probably why so many modern anglers prefer to sit behind ledger rods waiting for something to happen. Today I had a lovely letter through the post from one of our older anglers, a man named Frank Murgett. Frank is of the old school, but that does not mean that he is not an excellent fisherman. He has fished most of his life, has known many of the 'greats' and has had some super catches. To him fishing is an immediate, pleasurable and thought-provoking task, and this is what he has to say about the modern trend of ledgering: 'The invention of the buzzer has made a lot of fishing mechanical so that one does not have to pay attention and fish and watch. The buzzer today is made to catch bream and barbel as well as carp and the poor old tench to great size is often caught by accident. Yet, it will still count as being caught in the proper way.' Provokingly, Frank goes on to say, 'I think that I would have put a hammer through Walker's prototype buzzer had I had my way.'

Neither I nor Frank is saying that ledgering does not have its place sometimes, but for goodness' sake do consider the float first and foremost.

2 *Tackle for Float Fishing*

RODS

We must feel admiration for our grandfathers who used to float fish with most extraordinary long and heavy rods made out of various woods, bones and metals. It was not unusual in the 19th century for a long-trotting rod to weigh over 1lb, and some even approached 2lb! Add to that the weight of a big wooden centre-pin reel and you were talking about men with forearms the depth of bream!

Of course, rod materials began to refine quickly during the 20th century. Good quality split cane soon became the prized material, but by the 1960s this was overtaken by glass and then hollow glass. Hollow glass has proved an excellent material, but little by little this too has been inched out by the new carbon fibres. Today, carbon fibre is the acknowledged master of rod materials, but even this is developing all the time. Now we have lower resin carbons which allow the rod to be of lower diameter and to be made even lighter than they are already. So, the state-of-the-art float rod in the late 20th century will definitely be made of carbon fibre.

The next thing to look for in that perfect float rod is the difficult question of balance. This is hard to put into words, but basically the rod should not feel top-heavy. When you go to lift the rod it should come up cleanly without any strain or pressure on your part.

This is rather hard to comprehend, but in the tackle shop if you pick up a whole range of rods, both cheap and expensive, you will probably begin to see what I mean. Never choose a rod without taking your reel to the tackle shop. It is very important to put the reel on and to see how the two feel together. Even if the first rod you choose seems to fit the bill, try two or three more for comparison; remember, a good rod could well be with you for life.

The rod should also obviously be light – with today's materials this is not a problem. The lighter the rod – providing it is balanced – the longer you will be able to hold it without feeling any fatigue. Tiredness is annoying in itself, but it can also lead to mistakes and sloppy float control. The good float angler is always at the top of his sport and well in command of all his physical movements. Lightness obviously comes with slimness, and the thinner the rod is (all other things being equal) the better. A thin rod cuts through the air that much more cleanly and presents far less resistance on the strike or when mending the line. This is very important when fishing at range, for example, or in a high wind. Look at some of the old glass-fibre rods of the 1960s and see how enormously thick they were around the butt. Compare them to today's wand-like creations and consider how much easier the newer rods are to control in anything over a breeze.

When you are trying out a potential float rod you must feel that it is responsive and that it appears to be an extension to your own hand. You will definitely need to find a rod with a comfortable handle – this should be slim, and I still feel there is little better material than cork. The handle should not be too long, but neither should it be too short for this would also cause problems. For most adults, a handle of around 22–23in appears to be correct.

You must also check the rings of the rod. These should be of the best possible quality, the present market leaders probably being Fuji. Their rings are both light and hard wearing, and they allow the easiest possible passage of line. Cheap rings tend to be heavy and these spoil the action of the rod. They also become grooved easily as the line cuts into them, and in turn the groove can weaken the line disastrously, often at a crucial moment when a big fish is being played. Also, if the rings are not smooth then your casting distance is cut down dramatically. Even the science of ring-making does not stand still: titanium rings have now begun to appear on the market, but as they are extremely expensive it could be some time before they are seen on the average man's rod.

There is nothing about rod design that can be overlooked. Even the reel handle must suit you. These should not be heavy and yet they must grip the reel perfectly tightly to the rod handle. The reel should fit the rod as snugly as a bug in the rug, for if there is any wobble or play, especially when a big fish is on the line, disasters could emerge. Ideally, the reel must appear as if it is glued to the handle and will not budge under any amount of pressure.

A long rod is essential for good float control.

Obviously, the length of the rod is very important indeed – too often you see people struggling to control a float with a rod that is only 9–10ft long. For most people and for most types of float fishing, the perfect rod will probably be 12–13ft. If you choose one any shorter than this then you are cutting down the amount of control you will have over your float. There are now available longer rods of 14ft and even 15ft that are made acceptably light by the advent of the new carbon-fibre materials. A 15ft rod will give you quite a bit more control over your float and it is quite amazing how this extra length will pick up far more line on the strike. However, these longer rods are specialized tools and do cost an appreciable amount of money.

Another thing you will have to decide upon is the action you want from your float rod. Basically there are two actions, the first being a tip- or a forward action. With such a rod it is just the tip section that bends, whilst the middle and butt sections remain comparatively stiff and rigid. The tip-action rod is probably the favourite of most anglers – it allows a rapid strike and is perfect for close-in control, say when fishing the stick float. It probably also plays a fish somewhat more directly and allows you to keep a plunging chub, for example, very directly away from a snag.

The alternative to the tip-action is a rod with an all-through action. With this type of rod the middle section is much softer and there is a continuous bend all the way through the blank to the butt itself. Such a rod can feel a little bit floppy in comparison to the tip-action rod, and certainly does not feel quite as tight and delicate. However, it is perfect for fishing a waggler, say, at a distance when you have to move a lot of line through the water on the strike. Also, being softer, you do not tend to bump quite so many fish on the strike – the rather stiffer action of the tip-action rod can bounce a hook out of a fish's mouth.

The choice of rod is very much yours. There is no absolute favourite and every angler has his own personal preference. Probably the best thing to do is bear in mind some of the points I have made and go to a good tackle shop where there is a wide range of rods that you can try out. Do not buy anything that you feel in the least unhappy with and, if possible, try to borrow somebody else's rod on the bankside – even if only for a few minutes – so that you can feel it in action.

REELS

The float fisherman is faced with a choice of three reels – again there is no absolute right or wrong choice here and the final decision is up to the individual.

Open-Faced Reels

The most common type of reel is probably the open-faced fixed-spool reel. This is now the traditional tool of most coarse anglers and it works well for float fishing. In fact, most of the professionals prefer this for distance float fishing at least. The open-faced reel is probably the easiest reel to use for distance casting and speedy line recovery. So, if you are fishing a waggler at distance on a stillwater then there is little to beat the open-faced reel. Also, as the open-faced reel is quite happy with line strength of anything between 1lb and 25lb, it has enormous adaptability.

The open-faced reel does not, however, answer all prayers in all situations. During trotting, for example, there is that difficult and delicate problem of striking and then engaging the bail arm. Although it might only be for a second, there is always the chance of the line going slack. Experience teaches an angler to minimize this, but the mechanics of the fixed spool do cause a problem here.

Closed-Face Reels

The alternative to the open-faced reel is the closed-face reel. This reel is probably the one most often chosen by the professional for speed fishing when the float is used fairly close in. As a result, it is the perfect reel for the stick float fished a rod length or two out. It is also the perfect reel to use in a wind, for it totally eliminates the chance of the line blowing round the handle or the bail arm. This might not happen very often, but if you are in an important match this occasional catastrophe could cause you minutes and quite a lot of money. The closed-face reel is an excellent tool for precise, delicate work where the breaking strain of the line does not have to be particularly heavy. Any line heavier than around 3lb breaking strain should really be used in conjunction with an open-faced reel.

The closed-face reel is therefore for the speed merchant, and to watch an accomplished matchman use one is an education: he can even appear to be winding in and feeding at the same time when he uses it!

Centre-Pin Reels

The traditional reel of our grandfathers was the centre-pin. This reel almost disappeared for a time during the 1960s and 1970s, but it then began to re-emerge as a cult item of tackle to some extent. There is, however, far more to the centre-pin reel than mere pretension. For one, it is impossible to beat playing a fish on a centre-pin. The fixed-spool reel relies on gears, and these do detract from the feeling of a plunging fish which transmits the shock straight to the angler who is using the centre-pin. The centre-pin is also one of the most

A perfect float fisher's summer day.

delightful reels that can be used for trotting a float down the stream. A well-made, well-oiled centre-pin will revolve so responsively that even an easy paced river can peel line from it. All the angler has to do is concentrate on controlling the float and the reel will do the rest. Also, on the strike, there is no bail arm to flick over with the centre-pin: you are into the fish immediately and can play it instantly.

The centre-pin is still rather the terrain of the expert, and of the man who is quite happy with his tackle and his fishing. It is probably fair to say that in many river float-fishing situations the centre-pin is a reel that cannot be beaten – it is therefore well worth your while trying to obtain one and putting in the necessary practice. Elderly centre-pins are often advertised in the angling press and thankfully new centre-pins are being made again. They might appear expensive but they are wonders of mechanical engineering.

LINES

There have been incredible technological advances made in line development during the 20th century. Horse hair, cat gut and all the other various strange materials have gone for good, to be replaced by artificial nylon monofilament. The standard of line made today is extraordinarily good. When nylon first appeared on the market it was frequently unreliable and would often break way below its breaking strain. Not so today, and even the favourite lines of 1.7lb and 2.6lb breaking strains are virtually faultless in use. These two breaking strains probably account for ninety per cent of the sales in the UK amongst most anglers, but for the specialist angler 3.2lb breaking strain and 4.4lb breaking strain lines are probably more applicable. Anyway, it is up to you to decide on the breaking strain that your swim demands.

The important thing about a line today is that it should be durable and, especially, that it floats. A good line will have a fairly thin diameter which will allow it to come off the surface cleanly when you strike. This type of line does not grip the surface film and so the strike is that much more brisk and effective. Also, a line must come off the spool of your reel in a nice, orderly fashion. If it begins to twist or coil it will not float through the rod rings easily and it will impede the smooth passage of the float downstream. Bad line makes your job infinitely harder – discard it if you have any suspicions about it at all.

HOOKS

Hook choice again is very much a matter of personal opinion, and a great deal depends on the size of the fish and the type of swim you are fishing. You must try to choose a hook which presents the baits properly, but which is strong enough to land the fish when it is hooked. For this reason it is very important to study the wire gauges that are available in many hook sizes. If you choose a gauge too fine you will find that a chub will straighten it out; if you choose a gauge too thick you will find that the roach constantly avoid your bait.

Most of the best hooks today are made in Japan, although Mustad are world leaders. Hook manufacturers pay massive attention to detail and so must you. It is essential that the hook you choose is as sharp as possible, for very often you will set it at some range. Until quite recently hook points were cut, but now they are chemically etched which makes them much stronger and more durable. Also, microbarbs or even barbless hooks altogether are preferred today. This is partly because they are kinder to the fish, but also because a barbless hook presents a small bait like a maggot or bloodworm much more delicately. The

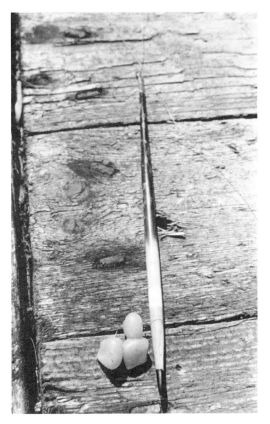

An old quill float with a modern forged hook.

even see their eyes. This is the sort of difference I am talking about – the wise angler probably has hooks of all sizes and knows just when to use them.

ACCESSORIES

One of the most important accessories when float fishing is good eyesight! Failing eyesight has been the downfall of many a top angler in the past. If your eyesight is not up to scratch then have your eyes tested – it could well be that you need glasses or contact lenses. I am not being funny here either! It is quite amazing how many people have eyesight problems and do not realize it. Fishing for a whole day and watching a float can be a very tiring, demanding experience, and if your eyes are not up to it you will end the session with a pounding headache.

Float fishing also demands the utmost in dexterity. If in winter your hands are cold you will simply not be able to work rod and reel properly. So, when temperatures plummet make sure that you have reasonable gloves, a hand warmer or a flask by your side at all times. Once that feeling goes from your fingertips then a great deal of your skill will disappear with it.

For many anglers, comfort is paramount. If they are not sitting at ease then their concentration wanes and their float fishing suffers. This is why you see most, if not all, match anglers enthroned on enormous padded boxes. However, I was not built like that and some of the great matchmen are not either – it is common to see anglers standing, crouching or positioned in any way that allows them to fish the most effectively. Do not be hidebound, but remember that fishing is a very personalized business and all that matters are your enjoyment and the amount of fish that you put on the bank.

barb rarely serves much useful purpose in stopping a fish getting off the hook and it is far better to contact more fish in the first place.

The whole question of hook sizes is an amusing one: if you ask a specialist angler what a small hook means to him he will probably say it is a size 14 or 16; ask a match angler what a small hook means to him and he will probably say it is a size 30! Most specialists use hooks between sizes 4 and 8, and it is a fair bet that ninety per cent of matchmen don't even own a hook bigger than size 12! Some match anglers have looked at my hooks and accused me of using grappling irons, but when they have shown me their hooks I could hardly

3 Stillwater Considerations

What you always have to consider with still-waters is that they are rarely, if ever still – even in the calmest of dawns when the surface is oily and the trees are reflected in perfect detail there is still some movement on the surface or just beneath it. And even on the smallest, most sheltered ponds and pits there will be some shift in the water, at least when the first breezes of the day begin to strike it. All this movement is caused by the wind, and it is this movement and the surface drag that it produces that causes some of the greatest headaches for the float fisherman. It has always been so, it will always be so and we have simply got to live with it.

The dynamics of stillwater movement are very difficult to understand. For example, whilst the surface layer might be moving one way, it is almost certain that the water at the bottom is moving in the opposite direction. If contraflows are difficult on motorways, then they make stillwater float fishing very problematic indeed! I suppose if the water at all depths was moving the same way then it would all pile up at one end of the lake! A mind-boggling concept, isn't it? I believe that there is a type of law attached to water movement that says that every action produces its own reaction. This means that if the surface is moving from left to right, then the chances are that the water at the bottom of the lake will be moving in precisely the opposite direction.

Obviously, the larger the water and the stronger the wind the greater this effect of action and reaction is likely to be. On very large expanses of water in winds that are blowing over force 4, it is possible to get a very thick surface layer on the move that may be 2–3ft deep which drifts steadily along even faster than a good many rivers. I clearly remember one day when I was fishing on a Scottish loch (an extreme example, but it makes a point) and a force 7 wind was blowing down its entire length. A bung cast from the bank at the bottom end of the lake travelled at a timed 5 miles per hour towards the outflow stream! Remember also that even when a wind drops its effect lingers on until the next blow comes along and strikes the water. Calmness is, in fact, virtually always an illusion.

The problem facing you when you are float fishing is that if you allow a float to drift around in this moving surface layer the bait presentation will suffer greatly. The baited hook will be dragged here and there along the bottom, but generally upstream against the current that is, of course, moving in a different direction. The result of this is that the bait behaves in a totally unrealistic fashion and no serious adult fish is likely to fall for it. Another problem is that sooner or later this moving bait is bound to run into bottom weed or debris, becoming fouled up and being perfectly useless.

ANCHORING YOUR FLOAT

It is almost impossible then to trot your bait in the same direction as the flow close to the bottom – the best that you can actually hope to do is to anchor your float and make sure that the bait does not move at all. This is probably the most important skill in stillwater float fishing and learning how to do it is the absolute key to success.

Sinking Your Line

Let us first look at what the line should be doing. A floating line simply makes control even more impossible, so you must sink it between the float and the rod tip. In fact, sinking the line is much more important than choosing the right float, for if it floats the drift

will build up on it and will exert so much pull that no float will be able to keep its position. There are several ways of going about sinking the line. First of all, it is important that you remember always to bury the rod tip after casting and tighten to the float by winding the reel handle. The deeper you bury the rod tip and the quicker you wind the handle, the more the line should sink – though you do not want to take this to extremes! Obviously, the technique to use is to overcast and then wind the float back into the baited area. When there is a great deal of surface drift you might have to overcast by anything up to 5yd or so to make sure you get the desired effect.

Now look at the line itself. Nearly all lines float to some extent unless given the treatment of sponging with a mixture of soapy water. I make my mixture up from washing-

Even on stillwaters as calm as this there will be some undertow.

up liquid, to which I add some water and which I keep in a little bottle. I then apply it to the line with a small sponge. I find that this method suits me, but it is common to read that Fuller's earth should be added to the mixture. This is available from chemists and comes in a powdered form. You simply add some of the powder to the soap and water mix, and hey presto! If it works better than my basic mix, then it really must be good.

Let us say that the wind is really fierce, the drift is appaling and none of these methods work. As a last resort to sink your line, add a dust shot to the line between the float and rod. In practice, this should be anything from 6in to 2ft behind the float – as a rule, the further away from the float, the worse the conditions. I would only recommend this as a last resort as there is no doubt that the dust shot does impede a strike to quite a great extent. Even so-called unmissable bites are missed, so it does pay to do without the shot if at all possible. Annoyingly, the worst drifts often occur when the surface is not really rippled. You seem to get a moving, glassy effect on the water and the line sometimes just refuses to move through it. At least when there is a chop this surface film breaks up and the line penetrates better. It is in these conditions that I often have to resort to the up-line shot.

Choosing Your Float

Back on the subject of floats, the key is to use an antenna-type float with the body at the bottom end. It is the thicker and more bulbous part of any float which will catch most of the drift, and the thinner bit that will catch the least. It makes absolute sense, therefore, to sink the bulk below the worst effects of the wind and the drift, and to leave the least affected antenna protruding through the surface for bite indication. Again, this is simply a result of understanding float design.

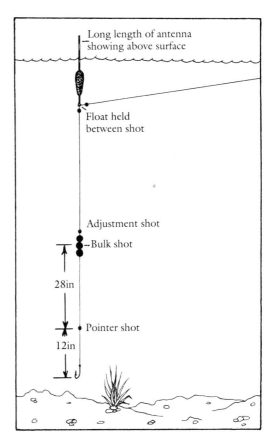

Fig. 1   Antenna rig.

Today there is an enormous range of these floats on the market, and the accomplished float angler will take quite a selection with him to cover all kinds of water and wind strengths. The golden rule is not to be afraid of weight and size. These floats are exceptionally well balanced and the important thing is to be able to cast over the fish and retrieve back to the baited area. If you use too light a float you will always be struggling. Put simply, there is no sense in cutting down on the size of the float when drift is bad, for the longer the float is and the further from the surface hangs the main body of the float, then the more control you will have.

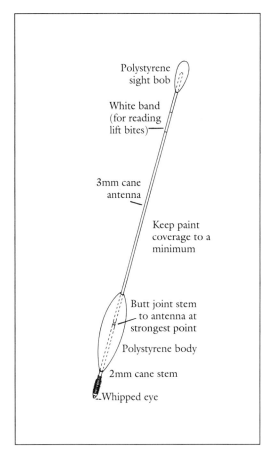

Polystyrene
sight bob

White band
(for reading
lift bites)

3mm cane
antenna

Keep paint
coverage to a
minimum

Butt joint stem
to antenna at
strongest point

Polystyrene body

2mm cane stem

Whipped eye

Fig. 2 Making a driftbeater.

Over the years there has been quite a range of floats designed in this way – large duckers, swingers, cocktails, missiles and, latterly and very successfully, driftbeaters. Their make-up has been much the same, and cane, reed or peacock have figured largely in the antenna part of the float, this section being anything from 6in to 10in long. The bodies of these floats have generally been constructed from balsa. Obviously, use those with the short and thinner antennae for close, fine work in calmer conditions and move towards the larger, heavier ones as the wind strength increases.

All this sounds excellent in theory, but in practice there are many occasions when the surface-water drift is just too deep and too strong for normal methods to combat it. Also, if you want to fish at great distances then the methods I have outlined so far probably will not be quite sufficient. In these situations the remaining option is to hold the float in place with an anchor shot. This can seem quite a drastic thing to do, but often quite a small shot – say, a size 6 – will serve to hold the entire rig in place. A size 6 shot looks rather small to be an anchor, but in actual fact that is what it is doing. The method is not unlike traditional laying-on, and all the standard antenna floats will do the job quite nicely. Antennae with thin tips will work to an extent, but when the conditions get really bad the float that is called for is one which has a fat tip – the ideal is the driftbeater.

The Driftbeater

This is the perfect float when using an anchor shot at distance or when drift is strong. It has a big, bulbous, bright top to it. These tops originally started out as a sight bob – that is, their size made them more visible at distance. It was soon found, however, that the sight bobs were also very effective at holding the float above the water. In fact, the sight bob was almost a buoyancy aid which enabled the float to rid the pressure of building drift.

Such is the buoyancy in the tip of a drift-beater that the anchor shot can be larger than a size 6 and the float will not be troubled. The actual positioning of this shot is very important, and generally it is somewhere between 6–12in from the hook – there are no hard-and-fast rules (are there anywhere in fishing?). However, if, for example, some of the bites you are getting are very quick, sharp and impossible to hit, this could mean that the shot is too close to the bait so that the fish is

A small water like this can build up severe current.

feeling the pressure and ejecting the bait immediately. Obviously, in this case you would move the anchor shot further away from the hook. If, on the other hand, you are reeling in crushed casters or sucked maggots and you have seen no real movement on the float, this means that the fish are taking bait well in, are moving around and then are spitting it out before you have been able to strike. In this case it would be advisable to move the shot closer to the hook and move the float down by the same amount to compensate.

The driftbeater is an interesting float to look at. Typically, it has most of its body weight down at the base, a very thin antenna that cuts down the effects of drift but then, and the most important feature of all, it has a little balsa body at the tip. The body is much fatter than any of the tips of traditional floats, and is buoyant enough to hold up on the surface and fight quite strong drift pressure on the line.

Brilliant as this float is, you still have to employ all the usual techniques with it – overcasting, burying the line, soaking the line in soapy liquid and even, on occasions, the use of the back stop. Also, never forget to tighten everything up so that there is no excess line which can drift around to form a belly. The more line there is in the water, the greater the pressure from surface drift and the more difficult it will be to control the float as a result.

The driftbeater is probably the perfect modern float upon which to register the lift bite – Fig. 3 really explains it all. It is important to sink the float right to the bottom of the sight bob. The anchor shot should be a single large one – use even a swan shot with the biggest driftbeaters available. It probably pays to put the shot about 2in from the hook. When a fish sucks in the bait, the float rises in the water and the coloured antenna becomes visible. This is quite useful for seeing how the

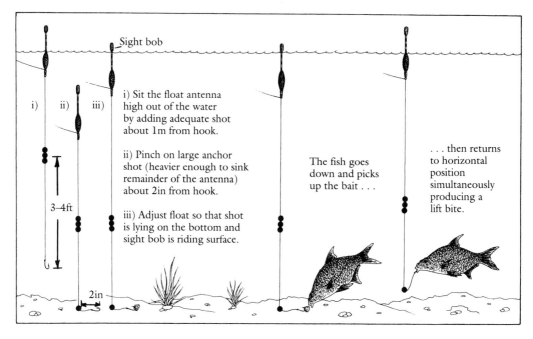

i) Sit the float antenna high out of the water by adding adequate shot about 1m from hook.

ii) Pinch on large anchor shot (heavier enough to sink remainder of the antenna) about 2in from hook.

iii) Adjust float so that shot is lying on the bottom and sight bob is riding surface.

The fish goes down and picks up the bait . . .

. . . then returns to horizontal position simultaneously producing a lift bite.

Sight bob

3–4ft

2in

Fig. 3   Setting up the windbeater rig.

bite is developing and helps you decide when to strike. Generally, it pays to strike as soon as the float has risen appreciably, but sometimes you might want to wait until the float turns over at an angle and even slides under. Generally, this extra waiting period is unnecessary and can lead to bait ejection. Again, the size of the bite can be regulated to an extent by moving the shot either closer to or further from the hook.

Of course, all fishing is about experimentation and experience. We have already established that, and these rules are merely guide-lines. Adapt and change as the conditions and the fish dictate, and always be aware of what is going on around you. If the wind gets up or if you need to cast further, then obviously you move to a larger float. If the wind drops or fish are moving closer in then you can afford to go lighter. It is pointless setting out to a water with a preconceived

method or rig in mind, but that said, it is amazing how many anglers arrive at a still-water with their rods already made up. How they can know where they will be fishing and what the water conditions will be like amazes me. You simply have to keep an open mind and fish to suit the developing conditions.

BITE INDICATION

I have been talking generally about coping with pretty grim conditions, but there are times when everything is rosy and you can concentrate on the vagaries of the fish themselves. One of the nicest ways to fish is with a very fine stillwater antenna float – rather like the Drennan range of Stillwater Blues. The thing about plastic is that it can be made very fine, and it is this thinness that actually magnifies the amount the float moves so that bites

A nice rudd caught on a slowly sinking bait.

become easier to see and easier to hit. In fact, a rule of float fishing is that the thinner the antenna, the more sensitive it will be – and as a result, the bigger the bite you can expect. There is a rough theory that a ½in dip on a 2mm-thick antenna equals a 1in dip on a 1mm-thick antenna. In other words, the bite is doubled simply because you have halved the thickness. That is the theory at least, and it seems to work well in practice.

In actual fact, you can leave quite a length of antenna protruding from the surface and this helps in deciphering very shy-biting fish. I suppose this is an advantage when dealing with small stuff, but I personally use this type of float a great deal in my quest for large crucians. Crucians, as we all know, can send anybody quite mad, but this type of float can work extremely well for them.

I have found that the light antenna is best fished quite close in – certainly not more than three or four rod lengths out – and it will cope with water up to around 10ft deep.

The length of antenna that is left clear of the water tends to slow bites down. I know that a matchman will dot the antenna right to the surface of the water as this is probably necessary for the small, shy, quick-feeding fish that he is after. However, for bigger tench or crucians this is not necessary. The two situations are quite different, and as the matchman is working against the clock he expects bites every cast and probably gets them. The man after bigger fish will probably have to wait twenty minutes or even a whole morning for a bite, but he does not want to miss it when it comes. This is where the slim antenna really comes in useful. The bite looks huge! It is slow, confident and seemingly unmissable. Very often these thin antennae also lean over at an angle so that you get a fair idea of the direction in which the fish is heading with the bait. This can be very useful with big fish in a tight, snaggy area.

It is virtually impossible to lay on with these floats as they are extremely sensitive and would soon be buried by the surface drift. I have found in the past that they work best if the bait is kept ¼–½in off the bottom – certainly the tench and crucians that I catch seem to like it that way. The float is also a nice one for taking good rudd close in on the drop. In these cases it pays to keep the bulk of the shot just underneath the float or fish the float with it trapped by a large shot on either side. This will ensure that the float cocks at once and the small shot down the line simply sinks it a little bit deeper when everything has reached the bottom. In fact, these antennae are so sensitive that you will actually see on the float the point when the hook and bait have gone down the full distance and settled. Obviously, if you count how long this takes you will know if a taking fish interrupts the process.

The driftbeaters that I discussed earlier are very forgiving floats. They will work well if the shotting is not particularly precise or sensitive, and they leave an enormous margin for error. However, this is not the case with the fine-tipped antenna float. The shotting on this float has to be absolutely spot-on or it will not work properly at all. Using such a float will mean a fair bit of fiddling around – often with very small shot – to get everything precise. A matchman will find that this pays off in terms of numbers of small fish that would win him money; the pleasure or specialist angler will find that he is amply rewarded by the single big fish that he is after.

The slim-tipped antenna is therefore the float to use when everything is tight, light and delicate, and it will only really work in calm or semi-calm conditions. If, after a calm dawn, the wind gets up and has a nasty bite to it, you will find that weed begins to drift and catch the line, and the antenna will sink over and over, giving false bites. You will then have to move to the less sensitive driftbeater.

4 *River Considerations*

Unlike stillwaters, at least on rivers you expect to find a current – although the recent rates of abstraction by water authorities have meant that sometimes they have been denied any flow whatsoever! Still, environmental worries are, I suppose, outside the scope of this book.

Perhaps the most traditional way of fishing a river is to trot a bait down with the current to where the fish are waiting. This method is centuries old and the float to use is the traditional Avon. However, as in all float fishing this is not quite as easy as it sounds. When trotting a swim there is always a tendency for the float to move across the natural flow of the river and work towards the bank from which you are fishing. This pendulum-type movement is completely unnatural and if you allow it to happen no decent fish will ever fall for the bait. The number one rule, therefore,

It always pays to get out in mid-stream for the best possible float control.

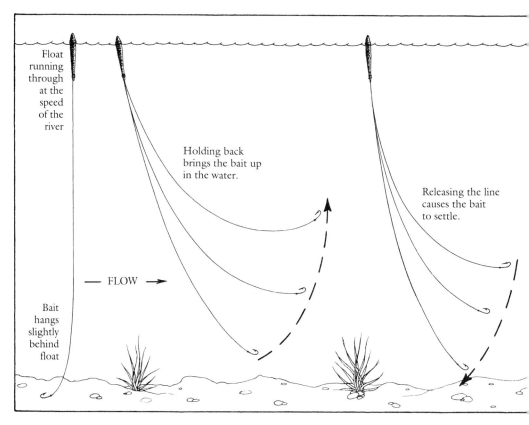

Float
running
through
at the
speed
of the
river

Holding back
brings the bait up
in the water.

Releasing the line
causes the bait
to settle.

— FLOW →

Bait
hangs
slightly
behind
float

Fig. 4 Holding back the stick float.

is that the bait should travel straight through the swim, following exactly the contours of the current that is speeding it along. To trot the river in such a way is very easy if you find a swim where the current goes directly away from you – as so often happens if you are on a small promontory or at the bottom of a bend. It is also easy to keep the float in a direct line if you are only trotting it beneath your rod tip. The trouble is, however, that not all swims accommodate such presentation, and frequently it is necessary to look for fish further out or across the river.

Certainly, it is stupid to try to fish the Avon more than a couple of rod lengths out – beyond that it is very easy to start struggling and losing control. Float control is also made a great deal easier if the line is fairly light – say up to 4lb. Above this breaking strain the diameter of the line tends to hug the current, create more resistance and be pulled off course. The new low-diameter lines do help in this respect, and with the double-strength varieties you can trot an Avon quite happily with a 5lb or even 7lb line at a push. An upstream wind is also very important and the Avon float hardly operates successfully at all if there is anything like a downstream wind blowing.

Another golden rule of rivers is that the current tends to move rather more quickly on the surface than it does towards the river bed.

Of course, this characteristic of rivers does not matter very much to the swimfeeder man, but it is of vital importance to the float fisherman. As most of the decent fish are deep down, what we have to try to do is get the bait moving against them at the same speed as the current is there, and not the same speed as it is on the surface.

This leads us to another rule: one of the major arts of trotting is to hold the float back slightly and so slow it down, thus allowing the bait to go in front of the float. This means that the bait is travelling at about the correct speed deep down and also lifts up enticingly through the water from time to time. The trout men call this the 'induced take', and there was a great deal of excitement among fly fishermen some thirty years ago when the use of this method was really broadcast – what the trout anglers failed to realize, however, was that good Avon float men had been using the technique for years.

This method of holding back is very easy when the current flows away from you or if you are fishing in a straight line beneath the rod tip. Obviously though, it gets far more difficult the further out you are fishing. There is no way you will hold back correctly when fishing even a couple of rod lengths out, unless there is an upstream wind which allows you to keep the line nicely behind the float.

So far I have talked about an upstream wind, but on those rivers that flow from west to east you might expect such wind direction to be quite rare. However, you do not have to wait for a precise easterly. Most of the time light winds tend to funnel along the course of a river, channelled by steep banks or trees. This means that they usually blow either up or down the river and the chances are that you will often be in luck.

The problem with a downstream wind is that the flow of water is speeded up, and this catches on the bulbous body of the Avon and

A downstream wind can be a problem.

PERFECT YOUR FLOAT FISHING

pushes it along faster than it would normally go. A wind blowing upstream, however, will work in exactly the opposite way and hold the float up for you without you doing anything yourself. Such is the importance of wind direction that you can see why pleasure anglers will often walk miles to find the swim that suits them best.

WHICH FLOAT?

The Avon

The Avon float has its body right at the top end and it should be shotted so that this bulky

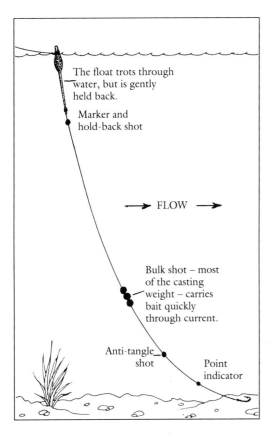

The float trots through water, but is gently held back.

Marker and hold-back shot

→ FLOW →

Bulk shot – most of the casting weight – carries bait quickly through current.

Anti-tangle shot

Point indicator

Fig. 5 An Avon rig explained.

bit rides just beneath the surface. This provides the horizontal stability that I talked about in Chapter 3, and it means that when you hold the float back it won't keep 'popping' out of the water, disturbing the bait beneath. Also, few rivers glide along as smooth as glass, most having little pockets of boils, eddies and turbulence that tend to pull under a float that is not fairly buoyant.

Traditional Avons have a cane stem and a balsa body, and are usually quite large, carrying between three and six BB. They can be fished in quite deep, fast water for they do have tremendous buoyancy. The diagram (*see* Fig. 5) explains most of what you need to know about the shotting patterns, but remember that the small marker shot is quite important to stop the float sliding down. The bigger stick float will also cope with larger baits – even fairly small pieces of luncheon meat or pieces of bread flake. All these attributes make the float perfect for species like chub in reasonably quick water.

The Wire-Stemmed Stick Float

The wire-stemmed stick float is really for smaller baits, slightly slower water and for swims that can be fished close in and very tightly. On small rivers or tight-in swims where roach, say, are feeding avidly on casters, the wire-stemmed stick float is hard to beat.

Again, the diagram (*see* Fig. 6) explains the perfect shotting pattern for this float. The shot is probably best strung out 'shirt button' style, and remember also that the wire stem acts as a keel and slows the float down on its own. The wire stem also gives the float quite a bit of stability and allows the angler to hold back quite hard without raising the float through the water. This is a perfect float, therefore, to work through a small swim very tightly when the fishing is difficult.

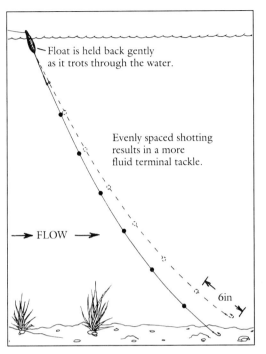

Float is held back gently
as it trots through the water.

Evenly spaced shotting
results in a more
fluid terminal tackle.

→ FLOW →

6in

Fig. 6   A wire Avon rig.

The Waggler

So what happens when you want to fish further out and/or the wind is blowing downriver? The stick, certainly, is virtually out of the question. By and large, if you are fishing at any distance or if the wind is not as it should be, then a waggler float is almost certainly the one to choose. A buoyant waggler, especially the type made out of peacock quill, is an excellent float for dragging the bottom. It has extra resistance and is that bit more difficult to pull under the surface. The difference between the waggler merely dragging under and a bite itself is something that you can only come to read through experience. However, when the bottom is responsible, the float tilts and gradually disappears from view, but when a fish bites everything is that much more positive.

A waggler is excellent for fishing the far bank (if the river is not too wide), especially if there is a noticeable snag or lie there. The best idea is to position yourself virtually opposite and cast slightly upstream so that the trot through is not particularly long – 4–5yd is quite long enough. The idea is to feed pretty consistently with a pouchful of maggots or casters, providing you are getting some indication from the fish.

Remember that in this situation your line is to some extent sunk between the float and the rod tip, and therefore a strike is best made by sweeping close to the water surface. Anything like a vertical strike will have to pull line up through the water so that a great deal of the power will be dispersed. Obviously, fishing long distances only increases the amount of sunken line that has to be lifted and this can often result in a missed or bumped fish.

A waggler will only cope with a certain amount of downstream wind. If the speed of the surface water really increases then there is the option of putting on a longer waggler. An extra 2–3in on the float will really work wonders in slowing it down. The trot through will take perceptibly longer and this, of course, leads to a much nicer bait presentation. On a small, clear river, however, there is obviously a limit to the length of waggler you can get away with. When the wind speed reaches difficult proportions, the way around it is to change the straight-bodied waggler for a bottom-end-only float with the weight down near the eye. These floats are given names such as duckers or zoomers, and generally have a reed or plastic antenna and a balsa body down deep. The thin antenna means there is little resistance to catch the wind and the bulbous body makes it slightly more stable. The body also allows the float to carry more shot which in itself increases stability, and the extra shot allows you to bait quickly to the decent fish and pass the small nuisance fish such as minnows, dace or bleak.

Of course, you do not necessarily need a downstream wind for either the long or short waggler, and life is much easier if the day is calm. If it is, then you need not even worry too much about sinking long lengths of line, thus making striking much more easy. Ideally, both floats can be used in water of up to 8–10ft in depth, and the shotting patterns illustrated in the diagram (*see* Fig. 22) are pretty good for starters. However, in the past when I have found bites a little difficult to hit, I have found that moving the two-trap shot further apart on the waggler system sometimes helps to cure the problem to an extent.

Balsa Stick Floats

These days the most commonly used river floats are the balsa stick types. These are attached top and bottom, and in the bigger sizes are particularly good on deep rivers where the flow is fairly smooth and tight control is important. The larger floats take quite a lot of shot but this is not a problem. A fish does not have to pull all the lead to make the float register a bite, but only has to take the bait in its mouth and stop the natural movement of the shot nearest the hook. When this happens the bite is seen – this is why the bottom shot can be called an indicator shot . . . after all, that is its purpose. Also, if you load most of the shot towards the bottom then you will find that the bait is pulled down quickly through the nuisance species. A good sized balsa stick float will not therefore be blown around in odd gusts of wind, and there is also a fair bit of weight to pull against when mending the line – something that is really important if you are to avoid the bait behaving unnaturally.

Shotting patterns are often seen as being very complex and it does pay to get them right. For example, with the big balsa it is important to have that indicator shot closer to the hook than to the bulk shot above it. Also, try and keep the shot nicely proportioned. If you are using BBs down the line, a dust shot will not really work as an indicator l. A larger shot will be needed (perhaps a number 4) so that there is a nice gradation down the line.

The long, slender balsa stick floats are very useful for stret pegging – a method which I describe later on in greater detail (*see* pages 68–69). This is a perfect method, especially in the winter when fishing the slack or slower swims. Remember to fish quite considerably overdepth with one or two smaller shots on the bottom so that the bait drags around. This will allow you to keep close control of the float and hold it back hard as it inches down the current, gradually moving in towards your own bank. This is a method that you have to fish close in, so extreme caution is called for – especially when you are after large, shy fish.

Stret pegging is a method that is made more difficult by a downstream wind which always wants to hurry the float through faster than you can allow it. This tends to be the case with all double-rubber-float fishing on rivers; as I have said before, when the river is subject to the downstream wind you probably need to start looking at bottom-attached floats for real control and stability.

For both rivers and stillwaters a great variety of floats is now available, one type often only duplicating another. Remember, too, that many floats are made to catch anglers, not fish. I know that this is said a lot but it is the truth. The important thing is to be able to read the river, the swim and the habits of the fish you are after and then put on the right float for the job. Thereafter it is experience again which comes into play: the ability to use the float to its utmost potential. When you get everything right, and the float goes under and a fish is hooked, then there are few things more satisfying in this super sport of ours.

5 Floats and Methods

This chapter introduces some of the more common floats and methods that any fresh-water angler is likely to meet. Not every float and method is contained within this chapter, but those that are not will be found later in the book along with the species for which they are most applicable.

THE WAGGLER

The waggler is really any float that is attached by the bottom only, as opposed to the stick float which is attached to the line at both top and bottom. The waggler is not really a particular float at all, rather it is a term applied to floats that can come in different shapes, sizes and materials. The one common denominator is that they are attached at the bottom end.

In general, there are two types of waggler: the straight variety; and the bodied variety that provides more stability in rougher conditions. The main part of the waggler float is generally made from either plastic, reed or quill, and if it is bodied then this is constructed from balsa or cork. Some wagglers have a thin insert at their top for greater sensitivity and this is made from thinner quill, plastic or a wisp of reed. Wagglers can be either very light (around 2BB) to the really big varieties (around 3SSG). There are now many companies making waggler floats and

most of them are absolutely excellent, such is the modern competition. Indeed, it is so easy now to go and buy an excellent waggler float that making them at home is really rendered unnecessary.

Wagglers are excellent for getting baits out a long way to fish and making sure that the tackle stays in the swim. As it is attached by the bottom end only and most of the shot is bulked around its base it flies rather like a dart. This makes extreme casting distances possible – even against a wind. Also, because the waggler is attached at the bottom end only the line to it from the rod tip can be sunk beneath any surface chop, again adding to its stability.

Choice of Waggler

A good angler assesses his swim very quickly and bears several points in mind when it comes to choosing the float. First, he assesses the location of the fish. If he wants to fish only four rod lengths out, then he will choose a light waggler which is able to carry around 3BB or 4BB shot. If bream are priming at 20yd or more in the distance, for example, you should opt for a much heavier waggler that will take several AAA shot or even 2SSG or 3SSG shot.

The important thing to remember is that it is foolish to fish a float that is too light. Modern floats are very well balanced, and it is far

A very slow-moving mill-pool – ideal for the stick float.

better to be able to cast beyond the fish and pull the float back in to the area than to struggle to make the distance in the first place.

The next assessment when choosing a float is wind strength. This is almost always a factor on large open stillwaters and the stronger the wind, the longer the waggler to be chosen. In fact, a long waggler can remain rock stable in even violent conditions, and a bodied waggler will also keep the bait that much more static. Once more, it is best to fish 'overlong' than 'overshort' – a float that is too light and too short will always be a headache and will always be wandering out of the crucial area.

Depth of swim is also a vital consideration. The waggler tends to bullet through the water on arrival and if the swim is very shallow it can virtually arrow the bottom, obviously spooking any big, cautious fish that are in the area. In these sort of conditions a bodied waggler is a great help, for a shorter float can be used while the shotting capacity remains high.

The experienced waggler fisherman will also know what sort of fish he is likely to be taking on the day. Large, hungry fish are quite content to pull down a normal waggler, but smaller and shyer fish might well give very tentative bites indeed. For these occasions an insert waggler is a necessity.

Of course, conditions do often change throughout the fishing session and it is often vital to change the waggler several times as the wind increases, decreases or swings around to different angles. For this reason, it is better to use a float adaptor than simply attach the waggler through the bottom ring. Adaptors can be bought ready-made from tackle shops and allow an instant change-over. They also allow the waggler to hang more freely in flight, which in itself increases casting distance.

Casting Wagglers

Casting the waggler is also all-important and it should be a gentle, though unhurried movement. If you really have to punch the cast out then the chances are that the waggler you have chosen is too light for the job and should be replaced.

There can be a problem with the waggler set-up in flight as most of the shot is bulked around the float. This means that the float precedes the hook in flight, and this is where the art of feathering the cast comes in. The knack is to put your finger on the spool edge as the float nears its destination. This gradually slows down the line that is released from the spool and holds the float back somewhat. The hook then overtakes the float and lands in the swim first with the float following close behind. Tangles are eliminated and because the float has been slowed down it tends to land with less of a splash – a very important consideration when using a large float in shallow water for shy fish.

It is almost always important to cast beyond the hot area in your swim. This is partly to avoid scaring fish that have their heads down over the feed, but it also allows you to sink the line between the rod tip and the waggler. Once the float lands beyond the

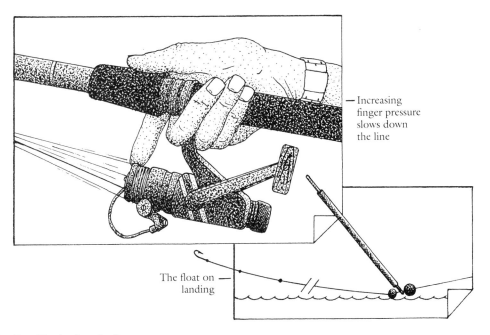

— Increasing finger pressure slows down the line

The float on — landing

Fig. 7   Feathering the line.

swim, sink the rod tip at once and reel in a few times sharply and jerkily. It also helps if you pull the rod tip under water, to either one side or the other. The waggler should bob up in the desired place with all the line sunk between its bottom ring or adaptor and the tip of your rod. Remember that even the slightest wind and almost insignificant flow will put the float away from the fish unless the line is well sunk. In extreme conditions a small shot nipped a couple of feet up from the float can be a blessing.

Bite Indication

At long range visibility is an important consideration and the float tip colour should be borne in mind. When the water is rough I prefer a red or an orange tip, but when the water is calm and the sky is reflected in it a great deal a black tip can be useful. Again, if the surface is very still and you are fishing under branches or in the reflection of, say, a building on the far bank, then a white tip might show up best of all. The choice of colour is important or severe eye strain can develop in the course of even a few hours.

Bites on the waggler are generally quite positive and the strike should be as steady as the initial cast. Avoid snatching at the bite or doing anything too sharply. A nice gentle lean into the fish is all that is necessary to set the hook, even at long range. Barbless hooks can be an advantage here as extra pressure is needed to take the hook past the barb.

River Waggling

Although I have talked mainly about wagglers on stillwaters, their use is also quite applicable to rivers – especially at distances greater than those that are easily handled by the stick float. Also, because the line is still generally sunk when fishing the river waggler, wind is not an

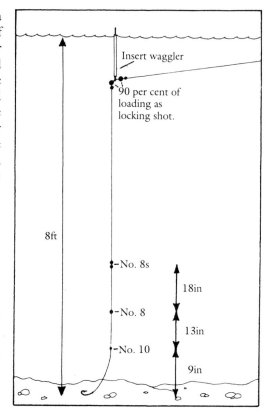

Fig. 8   An 'insert' set-up.

impossible obstacle to success. The worst possible wind for river fishing is one that blows downstream, but a waggler can handle even this. The basic problem for the waggler on the river is that it cannot hold the bait back in the manner of the stick float, and this can be a drawback on very cold days with, for example, big, shy roach.

All the rules for stillwater waggler fishing apply in rivers, and you will find that the light insert wagglers are excellent for slow rivers and smallish fish when bites are being looked for in mid-water. The bigger straight wagglers can be used when you want the bait to go down quickly in fast rivers like the Trent or the Wye, even when there is a lot of extra water in the winter.

The type of fish that every pole angler seeks – a small roach caught on bread punch.

POLE FLOATS

My own pole fishing is actually a bit of a cheat! There have been times on narrow East Anglian rivers when I have used a pole simply to give me better control over a very short trot or a long-distance laying-on approach. My own pole fishing, therefore, has been used in conjunction with the normal type of stick float, peacock quill or whatever. The intricacies of modern, match-fishing-type pole fishing are completely beyond me. For this reason I have enlisted the help of Kim Milsom in this section, who is not only one of the UK's leading match anglers but is also one of the lead-

ing pole fishermen. The following is his guide to pole floats:

'The whole question of pole floats is a confusing subject with so many patterns and variations being thrust at the potential consumer. If you are one of the puzzled punters, do not fear for a simple guide is here! Let's take this one step at a time, starting with the body shape of the float. This is probably the most important part of a pole float's design.

Body Shape

'The most universally usable shape is fairly wide in relation to its length, by which I mean it is either round or of a wide rugby-ball shape. This type of body offers good stability in rough conditions and is particularly useful in running water situations when the float needs to be held back. The water pressure on the wide upper section of the float seems to keep it pushed down in the river, whilst a narrow body would ride up far more, making bites difficult to spot.

'In still water or other situations where there is little need to hold the float back, an inverted pear shape (that is, having the widest part towards the base of the body) is also very good. This retains the stability associated with the wider float shape but also keeps a lot of the body slightly deeper in the water, helping to combat any surface flow.

'Obviously, there are many slight variations of body shape available, but if they fall within the guide-lines I have just given then the floats should be suitable. One or two specific exceptions to this body shape rule do exist – these are mentioned later in this section.

Stems and Bristles

'Now, let us have a look at stems and bristles. Cane, wire, fibreglass, plastic and carbon are all in regular use but which should be used and when? Here are a few of my suggestions.

'To start with, the diameter of the tip tends to hold far more importance than the material from which it is made. This can be proven if floats with bristles of the same diameter but of different materials are shotted down to the same point and then placed in a bucket of water. If you hit the top of both floats at the same time with the same amount of force, they will sink and rise in unison: this proves that their sensitivity is more or less identical and that tip material makes little difference.

'Wire is often regarded as the most sensitive material, but it is no coincidence that wire bristles tend to be of smaller diameter than their alternatives. A wire bristle is often little more than 0.5mm in diameter; this obviously makes it very sensitive, but for many people it is perhaps even too sensitive. Petroleum jelly often needs to be applied to the tip of such a float to prevent it from sinking, and surface tension can cause the float to set in an irregular manner. With these problems in mind, a beginner to pole fishing would be well advised to stick to slightly wider bristles of 1mm or more, which should be much more manageable. Plastic is probably the most commonly available tip material in these diameters but remember that other materials are also quite acceptable.

'Incidentally, it should be mentioned at this point that the tip of the pole float should not be left sticking out of the water by a couple of inches. If you are dealing with shy-biting fish, that is an awful lot of float to put under. It is far better to shot the float down as far as possible while still being able to see it. Tiny shot are obviously of great benefit when making slight adjustments to these very delicate floats. On fine lines, size 13 shot can easily be used to 'dot' the float down, and on many venues dotting the float down will lead to far more fish. It is certainly worth the initial hassle of getting things absolutely right. As well as fooling more fish, dotting the float down has a second big advantage: it puts the float body further below the surface, thereby keeping it away from the influence of both wind and surface drift. This, of course, helps to provide a more natural presentation of the hookbait. A third advantage occurs in running water when the float is held back hard. If the float starts to rise in the water, more bristle shows and the rig remains remarkably sensitive. If all of the bristle is showing to start with, holding back can bring part of the float's body into view and this will definitely make the whole rig much less sensitive.

The River Wensum in Norwich – often attacked with the pole.

Float Stems

'Moving on to float stems, wire probably gives the float maximum stability. However, a lighter stem will allow far more weight to be used further down the line which again will provide a stabilizing effect. This situation means that choice of float-stem material is often down to personal preference. However, for fishing 'to hand', a lighter stem will cast more smoothly as it follows the weight rather than trying to overtake it. Also, for fishing in very shallow situations a heavier wire stem will stabilize the float whereas the extra shot and line on a cane stem float could be prone to tangles.

'These are the basics of float design, so let us now move on to shotting patterns.

Shotting Patterns

'This subject can be broken down into two basic types. First let's start with the most widely used olivette and dropper system.

'When the fish are feeding at a fairly specific depth – often on or near the bottom – the use of an olivette or bulk of shot down towards the hook is the most efficient way of getting the bait to their level. The positioning of the main weight will vary with the type of bait being used and how varied is the depth in which the fish are feeding. However, the lead is usually between 18in and 4ft from the hook. The shorter settings are usually used for delicate baits such as lugworm which will quickly be sucked dry and discarded by fish if the bite does not register virtually immediately. The 18in setting for the olivette or bulk shot is usually complimented by one or two small shot situated 6–8in from the hook. These shot will be capable of registering on the float bristle – if they fail to register or are lifted a bite is quickly seen and struck.

'The longer olivette settings are usually used with tougher baits such as maggots and normally include three or four small shot below, starting 12–18in from the hook and then at 6in or 9in intervals back towards the olivette. This kind of shotting will not register bites quite so instantly, but it will allow a more natural fall of the bait through the catching zone which in turn should lead to more bites. Obviously, if the bait is mangled without a bite registering, it is time to consider moving the weight closer to the hook.

'The second main type of weighting used in conjunction with pole floats is a string of small shot spread down the line which enables the angler to catch fish at all depths on the drop. In a river situation this is almost identical to stick float fishing, but the use of a pole means that excellent float control can be maintained at much greater distances from the bank than an ordinary rod would allow, especially in a strong downstream wind. Strong flows obviously limit the efficiency of this style and fish which drop down the peg cannot follow, but it is a deadly approach in steady currents. Shotting normally starts 12–18in from the hook and number 8 shot are usually used, with number 10 shot closest to the hook. Float size obviously varies with depth and flow as it will for all methods. If you cannot control the float then put on a bigger one!

'In canals or stillwaters the shotting for fishing on the drop will usually revolve around number 10 shot or even smaller as there is no appreciable flow. But the same spread shot principles apply and, when fish are feeding at all levels in the water, this shotting can certainly outscore the more limited olivette approach.

The Dibbler

'Earlier I mentioned exceptions to the normal pole float rules. The main one worth mentioning is usually known as a 'dibbler', and comprises a peacock quill body with no bristle and a fairly short wire stem. These are used for fishing overdepth, often in shallow water – for example, on the far bank of a canal. By fishing overdepth, often with one or two tiny shot on the bottom, this float is anchored in position rather than held there by the pole. The flat top provides enough extra buoyancy to prevent the float from dragging under, and this method of presentation when the fish demand a still bait on the bottom can be superior to a standard bristle float. Dibblers are especially useful in windy conditions, when holding a bristle float completely still at long range is no easy task for any angler.

'A larger version of the same float (this time very much like a stick float) can be used on rivers to achieve the same overdepth presentation where a bristle will continually drag under. I should also mention here that with all sizes of this float a string of shot is normal, rather than an olivette or bulk shot.'

Hopefully this basic guide will help you make more sense of the forest of pole floats which are now available in tackle shops; choosing the right ones and using them to maximum effect should now be a little easier.

SLIDER FLOATS

Today's slider floats are comparatively delicate when compared to the earliest versions. One of the first references to slider floats that I can find is in the book *Coarse Fish Angling*, written and published by J. W. Martin (the 'Trent Otter'). He wrote back in 1908:

'Many years ago, I remember, a question was asked in one of the sporting papers something like this: "Can a twenty-five foot deep swim be fished with an ordinary eleven foot rod, and if so, how?" The answer to that printed at the foot of the quest amused me. "It is an impossibility, unless the angler had a big tree and a long ladder at his back, so that on hooking a big barbel he could mount the tree whilst his companion below landed the fish."

'It is said that "Nottingham George" was the inventor of the slider float. There was a very deep, shelving hole down the Trent and, do as he would, old George could not properly fish it, though he knew it contained quantities of fine barbel. He said afterwards the idea of putting rings on his float and a stop on the line at required depth came to him in a dream; and so he worked the idea out with a big, long corking float and after one or two experimental trials he succeeded in making what we suppose to be the first slider float.'

The sliding float that Martin did go on to describe was built for him by Charlie Hudson:

'The float that this old angler had just put in my hand was a swan quill ten inches in length. Then four or five new corks had had a hole burned lengthways through them; these corks were fitted together and glued up close and tight with some waterproof cement, the cork portion being about six inches long, and two inches of quill projected from each end of the cork; each end of the cork was tapered down to the quill and it was two and three quarter inches in circumference at the thickest part; the cork was filed and sandpapered smooth, finally being coated with a little enamel and a brilliant dab of scarlet vermilion on the end that projected above the water. The peculiarity of this float was in the rings that mounted it; there was an upright rod ring about three eighths of an inch in diameter just above the top end of the cork and another very tiny upright ring just below the bottom end of the cork, the lower or latter ring being very small indeed, in fact, only just large enough to

A really big river that can demand really big floats.

permit a small darning needle to go through it. This float was wanted to fish that very deep and heavy stream, and also with our eleven and a half feet barbel rod. I remember when we sent that float on its trial trip it carried eight or ten very large split shot and also two heavy pipe leads at least two inches long each of them.'

Martin then went on to explain how the float could be set according to the depth and stopped by a knot using a tiny piece of elastic or a quarter length of string on the line. The stop knot would pass easily through the rings on the rod but would not pass through the smaller of the two rings of the float. Obviously, the float would slide up and down the line but would then be fixed by the stop knot

at the required depth. The development of this float revolutionized Martin's catches and he describes one particularly good day when the float kept burying at 70yd distance in a 20ft-deep swim. Just playing a 5lb fish took twenty minutes in such water and by the end of the day Martin was absolutely exhausted. The method had been found and it worked – as I am sure it would to this day.

This all brings to my mind a particular swim on the River Wye that is something over 20ft deep and very quick even in low conditions. The barbel live in the swim in great number and swimfeeder fishing does do well. However, I am quite convinced in my mind that a moving bait would sort out better fish that are becoming wary of the stationary bait. Charlie Hudson's enormous float is just the type of thing that I need. Whether I will ever have the courage to build and use such a creation I sometimes doubt. But then again, it would be an exciting thing to attempt, and surely what our grandfathers once did we can emulate today.

Modern slider-float fishing is by comparison a tame if very efficient affair!

The diagram (*see* Fig. 9) explains the ideal shotting patterns for the modern slider float and learning to tie the slider knot is not at all difficult. Most antenna floats work well as sliders, especially if they have a decent body – for example, a driftbeater float or a zoomer float. One important point is that they must have a small eye. A swivel float attachment is a good idea for the slider float as the eye is so small that it will not allow any stop knot to pass through it.

In theory, there is no limit to the depth of swim that can be fished with a slider, and certainly 25ft is not beyond it. However, it pays to start fishing the slider on shallower swims, even only 6ft deep, to build up your confidence for the times when deep water has to be tackled. One point to consider is that a slider, once working, makes casting much easier no matter how deep the swim is. Before the cast, the float slides down the line to sit on the bunched shot. When you cast, therefore, all the weight is concentrated in one area and it really arrows out very easily. This is one great advantage to using a slider float even in shallow water: you will find it is possible to fish the slider at very long distances and it casts well even into a strong wind. A second advantage is that the strike is made much more cleanly, especially at distance. What you are doing is striking through the bottom eye, and therefore you do not feel the float at all before the fish is hit.

There are a few tips that make fishing the slider a little easier. Sometimes, when really punching the slider out in difficult conditions, the float can tangle with the bulk shot if it

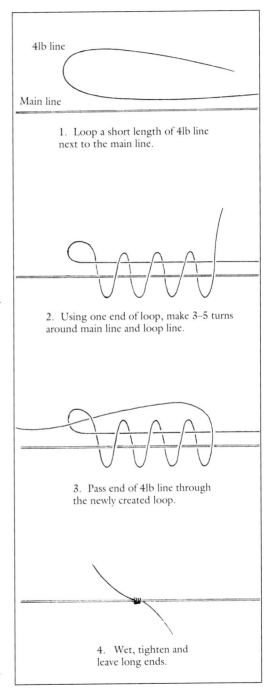

1. Loop a short length of 4lb line next to the main line.

2. Using one end of loop, make 3–5 turns around main line and loop line.

3. Pass end of 4lb line through the newly created loop.

4. Wet, tighten and leave long ends.

Fig. 9   How to tie a stop knot.

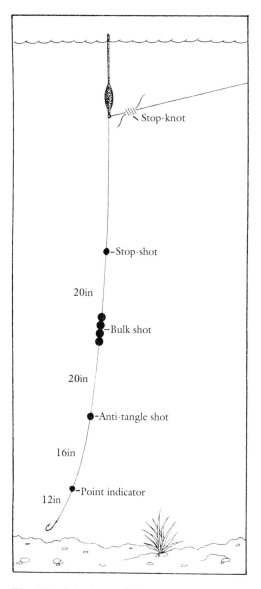

Fig. 10 Slider float – for long distances and rough water.

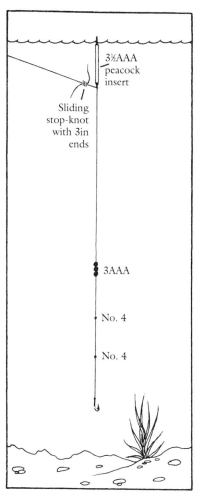

Fig. 11 A sliding float rig.

rests upon them. For that reason it often pays to put a small shot about 5–6in above the bulk shot on which the float can rest. This generally sorts out the problem. You will also notice in Fig. 11 that an anti-tangle shot is placed closer to the bottom shot than the bulk shot. This prevents a back tangle when a vigorous cast is made.

The final diagram (*see* Fig. 12) shows how to find the depth of a swim if you wish to fish the bait on the bottom. A BB is all you actually need, and this is a much easier way of doing things than using the usual plummet. Simply adjust the stop knot until the float is sitting properly – you then know that the BB is just off the bottom and the bait will be presented nicely.

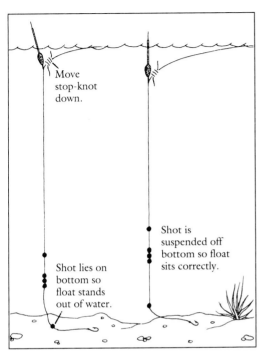

Fig. 12 Depth finding with the slider.

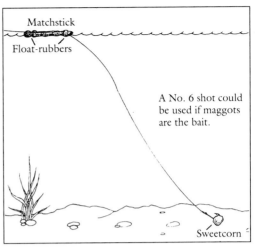

Fig. 13 A simple matchstick rig.

DIBBLERS

It is always amusing to realize that there is nothing new in angling at all. A fairly recent range of floats has been introduced, called, I believe, dibblers. They are very short pieces of peacock feather around 1in long that can be used close in on a running line or on the pole. Pole anglers in particular regard them as floats for larger fish. I say that there is nothing new in angling for the dibbler is really only a mass-produced, factory-made version of what we as boys used to find along the canal bank. In those days, thirty odd years ago, it was well recognized that the very shy roach of clear, shallow canals were frequently suspicious of a normal float and something very small and unusual could often work magic.

Generally, therefore, I remember arriving at the canal and rooting around amongst the grit for a reasonably intact matchstick! For obvious reasons, a floating matchstick was viewed with no alarm whatsoever and fish never bothered to give one a second look. Also, matchsticks are very light and incredibly sensitive to the smallest nibbling gudgeon. It was rare that a matchstick could not be found, but a twig from a branch would do nearly as well. In fact, in some swims matchsticks themselves became taboo and twigs were a necessary development.

A lot of my fishing is still done on slow or still clear waters where large fish are incredibly tackle-shy and there is still room for the dibbler. I do not actually possess any factory-built ones myself and the matchstick, a time-honoured tool, still does me well enough. Attached bottom end only or at top and bottom it is rare that a fish even notices it. Certainly, a matchstick lands virtually like thistledown.

Shotting is optional. Generally, I use a matchstick simply as a sight aid and allow the bait to drop quite naturally with its own weight. Very occasionally a number 6 shot will help with casting or will pull a small bait

Big bream like this are very difficult to outwit.

quickly down past surface-feeding small fish, but the addition of weight is very rare.

The matchstick once almost worked a miracle for me in my adult years; I was only used to it working wonders as a boy! The Railway Lake in Norfolk was always famous for the home of Eric, the gigantic mirror carp. Also present, however, was a very large, solitary stillwater bream. Quite often I tried to catch that fish but it was far too cunning for me and was obviously wary of tackle. Possibly it had fallen by mistake one night to a bottom-fished bait, but I always fancied catching it by stalk-

ing, for it was very visible during the daylight hours in such clear water. Very occasionally it could be tempted into taking a particle bait slowly on the drop. I remember that it liked casters which were rather orange and very slow sinking or the occasional maggot.

One particular August day the bream seemed more active than usual – possibly because there was a little wind on the water and the day was grey and heavy. It had taken three or four maggots but every time a float appeared it was away. I could not freeline a maggot because visibility was not quite good enough, and so I hunted out the old, traditional matchstick. Minutes later the wood cocked, travelled 3in to the north and sank. I struck and a great dustbin of bronze heaved 3ft beneath the surface. And then nothing. I reeled in and found that the maggot had bent neatly over the point of the hook, shielding the fish from the strike. Stupidly, I had not nicked it by the skin but had buried the point into the head. It had been a foolish thing to do and I felt betrayed by my excitement. But the float had worked. After all those years a discarded matchstick had once again shown just what it could do.

Make no mistake, certain big fish in clear waters sense the shop-bought float and a discarded piece of wood or twig from a bankside tree is just the thing to allay suspicion.

BUBBLE FLOATS

The bubble float has long been replaced in most anglers' bags and boxes by the more modern controller floats. All the bubble float ever did was to give added casting distance to pieces of crust or lighter baits. Of course, the bubble float was – and still is – based on an ingenious design, and the concept of adding water to give great weight is a clever one.

It does occur to me that particularly shy carp that have seen controller floats over most of their lives and have learned to become wary of them, no matter what design or colour they are, might well feel more easy around a bubble float. This is not based on pure hypothesis. I have tried bubble floats recently on heavily fished floater carp waters and have found them to work very well. Carp are never afraid of a bubble float – in fact, one of the problems I have had is trying to stop them attacking the float itself and eating it! The same remains true today and it was rather heartening to see that swirl once again at the float itself. Such a thing certainly does not indicate fright! So, although the bubble float is not an essential part of any man's kit it is a very useful addition on certain, be they rare, occasions.

FLOAT ATTACHMENTS

Attaching the float to the line is not always as easy as it may seem. There are varying degrees of sophistication and methods that can be used.

I suppose the simplest and probably the most cumbersome is to tie the float to the line! This, however, is only necessary in the most obscure situations when, for example, you are stalking carp and there is a need to use a twig, matchstick or something similar to act as a float in a newly developed situation. I can think of many times in my career when I have

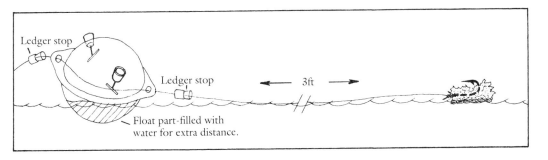

Fig. 14 A bubble float floating crust rig.

been creeping around the bank happy to free-line, when suddenly I found that a float was necessary. A slither of alder or willow has virtually always done the trick, and a simple knot has sufficed to keep the branch on the line for a short cast and a limited period of time. This is not to be recommended though for the more sophisticated methods of float fishing!

Stick floats or anything attached top and bottom as with Avons are held in place by float rubbers. These should fit very snugly indeed, and should preferably be new and taut. Older rubber tends to get slack, becomes cracked and snaps easily. The bands should not allow the float to slip during the cast or on the strike. Equally, sometimes the bands can fit too tightly (especially when using balsa Avons) and force the line to

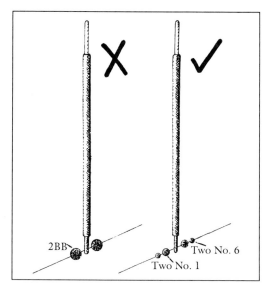

Fig. 16 Splitting up the locking shot.

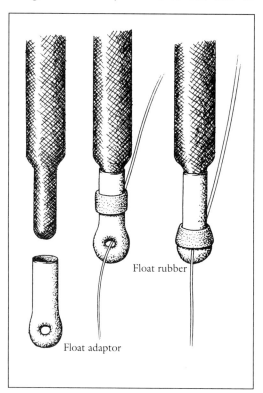

Fig. 15 Use of a float rubber.

groove the float and destroy its impermeability. Sometimes, when using a big Avon float at some distance, there is too much pressure for simple bands to keep the float permanently in position, and in these cases a small shot underneath helps stop the float from riding down the line.

With bottom-end-only floats – generally the wagglers – the line goes through the bottom eye. Sometimes, when I use a loafer-type float and do not want to use trapping shot, I loop the line two or three times through the bottom eye to keep the float in position. This works quite adequately but you have to be careful that the float is held securely. If it moves up and down the line it does tend to curl it and very quickly weaken it. This is especially the case with the new, thin-diameter lines that are prone to rapid weakening.

Obviously, the line is generally simply pushed through the bottom eye once and trapping shot on either side lock the float in position. This is the traditional way of setting a waggler float and it works very well. Care, however, does have to be taken when nipping the shot on to the line. Choose the softest shot possible and do your level best to make sure that the line is not nipped or weakened in any way. If very large shot are being used and the float is expected to undergo quite a lot of pressured fishing, tiny sleeves of silicone rubber can be placed around the line for the shot to grip. These tend to cushion the line and protect it during casting and striking.

Take care when moving the trapping shot up and down the line. It is far better to open it up with a nail or knife than to try to slide it. Sliding trapping shot up and down fine line is bound to weaken it – often very dramatically and with resulting dire consequences. If bites are being missed on the waggler it often pays to move the trapping shot a little further apart, say around 1–2in. As a general rule, when waggler fishing around eighty per cent of the weight is in the trapping shot and twenty per cent down the line. However, as I say, this is only a general rule.

There is one major problem with this method of float attachment: if for any reason the float has to be changed then the tackle has to be taken down altogether. For this reason, various float attachments have been developed that sit on the line and into which the float is pushed. Several of these are now on the market and all work very effectively. The most obvious and simple way is the use of a small silicone tube. When the tackle is being set up the silicone float attachment is put on the line between the trapping shot. The waggler float is then eased into the silicone tube, and if it needs to be replaced it is simplicity itself to take it out again. Nothing could be easier than the silicone float attachment, but you must always change floats with care or the line can cut through the silicone eye. I find it best to grip the silicone sleeve between my thumb and first finger, and then work it down with my nails until the float comes free.

Pulling will simply harm the float and possibly cut through the silicone eye. Good though the silicone eye is, not all big floats will fit in snugly and this type of attachment also means that the float stands out at an angle from the line rather than collapsing neatly on to it. This obviously has its effect during casting and on the way in which the float settles on the water.

Another device is the swivel float attachment. This is very similar to the silicone idea and indeed incorporates a piece of silicone tubing that embraces the bottom of the float. A tiny swivel is built into this, and the line

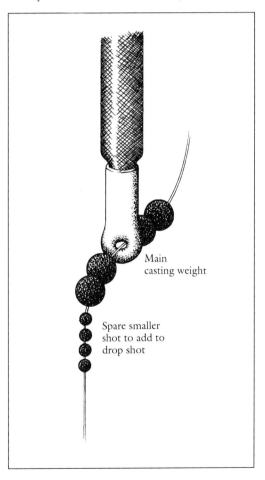

Fig. 17 The float adaptor.

The sort of swim that can be ledgered and that is also best fished with a float, taking the bait towards the raft.

runs through the eye. This is another useful method, but remember that the tiny swivel itself acts as a small weight. The eye of the swivel is of very low diameter and this makes it perfect for use with slider floats – it prevents any stop knot from passing through, however fierce the cast or the strike.

Very recently, Drennan brought out what probably represents one of the most important steps forward in float attachment. This is the link float attachment and has taken some twenty years to develop. The great thing about the link float attachment is that the line is kept absolutely straight and the float hangs perfectly from it. If a very big float is used then a small locking shot will prevent the sleeve from moving down the line. When depth changes are required the attachment slides up and down the line extremely easily. In flight the float sits exactly on the line and it also folds perfectly on the strike. The whole concept is very ingenious and it really is just about the ideal float attachment in a great number of cases.

A FLOAT IN THE NIGHT

During autumn and winter the fishing can be very hard during the daytime, especially when waters are clear and the sky is bright blue with brisk, crisp sunshine. It is these sorts of conditions that make most freshwater fish feed almost exclusively either just before darkness or for a couple of hours afterwards. Bits and pieces may be picked up through the daylight hours, but the real bonus fish will come when the sun has gone and the owls are about.

Most fish will feed at night.

Generally, whenever an angler thinks of night fishing it is with ledgering in mind. The usual procedure is either to quivertip or, on stillwaters, to use a glow bobbin at the butt, perhaps in conjunction with Optonics. Admittedly, in many situations the ledger works very well but there are numerous times when a float is much more efficient.

When Float is Best

This is best demonstrated with the following examples.

Example 1

A small estate lake holding some big roach. The lake is approximately 4 acres in extent, quite shallow and generally very clear. During the daytime the roach are very nervous indeed and even at night like to feed under cover. For this reason the best swim on the lake appears to be beneath the branches of a spreading horse-chestnut tree. The roach come in very close to the bank to feed, and almost under the rod tip – providing there is no bankside disturbance. To ledger this swim would be quite difficult as the weight would only be a few feet from the end eye. A float would therefore be a much more delicate and precise way of presenting the bait.

Example 2

A large, shallow lake holding a big head of medium to large bream. This water is approximately 20 acres in surface area but rarely deeper than 2ft or, at the most, 3ft. The shallow water makes the bream very wary of feeding during the daytime, and it is only after dark that they begin to patrol and look for food in earnest. They wander in large shoals, often fifty to a hundred strong, and once they find a baited area they really get their heads down. It is tradition to ledger for these fish at night, but the shallow water and the amount of broad-sided fish mean that line bites are a constant problem. It is very easy to strike again and again at false bites, thereby unsettling the shoal. Indeed, the bream now do not even like to feel the line along their flanks. In this lake it is much better to float fish at night as the line to the float lies on the surface, well away from the feeding bream beneath.

Example 3

A slow-moving river where the chub are particularly cautious. This river is typical of lowland Britain in that it moves very slowly apart from at times of flood. It contains a good head of big, old, wise chub that have seen every trick in the book. A static bait is a red alert to them and even at night, when they feed with confidence, they will only really accept a moving bait. This is when a float-fished bait really comes into its own as the flake, maggots, bread or whatever can be trundled very slowly through the swim.

These are three examples, but there are many more when the fish of your choice really wants a precise and delicate bait presentation that ledgering does not readily provide – and, of course, there is nothing to beat the thrill of seeing a float dip beneath the surface. I think everyone would agree that it is much more satisfying than seeing a bobbin rise or a tip flick round.

A Light in the Dark

There are three major ways of fishing a float at night: with a Drennan Night Light; with a Betalight; and with a white-painted quill or waggler float.

The Drennan Night Light is a tiny plastic cylinder that you bend until the internal glass breaks. You then shake it to mix the chemicals contained inside, and these provide a very bright glow. This cylinder plugs into all Drennan Insert Crystal floats and does not upset their balance or action at all. Nothing could be simpler – in seconds you convert a conventional float into one that is easily visible at night, certainly up to 10yd or more.

The advantages of the Night Light are many, mainly stemming from the fact that it is easy to use and is very highly visible. Also it is very cheap so that even if the float and Night Light are lost, no lasting damage is done to the pocket. The disadvantage is that the Night Light only really lasts for one full night session – say, around eight hours once the seals are broken. If you really get the night bug then they do work out expensive. They are, however, an excellent way of finding out if you like the method.

The second method is to use a Betalight instead of the Night Light. These are very similar in size and shape to the Night Lights, and just like the Night Lights the Betalights fit into any Drennan Crystal floats without altering their balance or performance. All decent tackle shops sell Betalights which generally come in different power ratings of 300, 400 or 500 units. I confess that I tend to use 300-unit Betalights and find that these are virtually as powerful and visible as the 500-unit type. The major difference between the Betalight and the Night Light is that the former lasts virtually forever rather than for one single session. This is their main advantage, and if the night-fishing bug really gets you then they are a very worthwhile investment. The disadvantage, of course, is that if a big fish breaks free then you have lost a fair amount of money.

The third way of using a float at night is to paint a quill or waggler float white with either liquid paper or white paint, and then fish it directly in a torch beam. This method does

work quite well and the cocked float will be very visible up to 25yd, providing the beam is powerful enough. There are obvious disadvantages however. If the water is clear and shallow, it is possible that the beam on the surface will actually scare fish from the swim. Also, during a long session torch batteries begin to wear down and the float will become more and more vague in the gathering darkness. It is also very annoying when a dithering bite takes the float out of the beam and into invisible darkness.

My own recommendations would be to start with a Night Light, and if you think you are going to like night fishing then move to a Betalight as soon as possible. I would reserve the final method for distance fishing in murky water.

Night Tips

Choose the weather for a night sortie carefully. Try to avoid very windy nights as the float will dance around so that you will soon be seeing double if not treble. The very best type of night is one that is fairly still, reasonably mild and overcast. In fact, the darker the night is, the more the Betalight or Night Light will show up.

Without the gift of sight, it is vital that you know instinctively where everything that you need lies. There is nothing worse than kicking over a box of maggots in the darkness, sticking a hook into your thumb or putting your foot on some precious floats. Get to the swim before nightfall and lay everything out neatly so that it is to hand when you need it. Winter nights can also be very cold, with a sunset often bringing about a falling frost. Do not neglect thermal boots and good warm clothing, and remember that a hot flask does wonders for numb fingers and falling spirits.

Sadly, we live in an increasingly violent and lawless age. On some waters it obviously

Big roach adore the hours of darkness.

makes sense to fish in pairs for your own personal safety. Also be careful that your car is parked in a place where there is some light and where it will be difficult to vandalize it. Fishing should not be about this kind of thing, but I feel duty bound to mention it.

There are a couple of further points worth mentioning when fishing at night. You might find that after a while of looking at a glowing float in the dark your sight goes blurred. It is easy to imagine that you are getting bites when in actual fact you are not! The tip is not to look at the Betalight itself but instead to focus to one side of it. That way the float is just in the corner of your vision and you notice when it disappears much more easily.

The big question often is how long to stay at the swim. This varies according to your own staying power and your gut feeling: if you really believe that there are fish about then it obviously makes sense to stay. I personally would be very loath to leave a swim where I was getting line bites or seeing fish top. However, if you are really miserable, cold and nothing at all has happened then it is just as well to remember that fishing is for fun and to go home. However, I've often found that roach in particular will feed at some time in the night, however cold it is. When I was younger and had more staying power it was not unusual for them to come on even at midnight.

Few people fish for pike after dark and they miss a great deal. It is quite possible to float fish for pike, the drifter floats showing up particularly well in a torch beam. The first couple of hours of darkness see pike on the rampage – especially in hard-fished waters where they are used to being caught in the daytime only.

Final Encouragement

Gunton Lake was fishing very badly for September. Very few bream had shown up and mostly only small roach were being caught. Danny and David were staying at my flat in the park and had permission to fish for a few hours after darkness. That alone was promising, but then they found that a large number of big bream were coming in to the deep north bank. Right under the rod tip, there is around 4ft of water and the fish were using this trough to feed along. Probably what attracted them in was the amount of loose feed that the daytime anglers had left behind.

Ledgering was a distinct possibility but the fish were so close that presentation would have been difficult. Also, there would have been more line in the water and the chances of line bites would have been greatly increased. The bream were fidgety and false striking would have served to drive them out of the trench sooner rather than later.

The obvious answer was to float fish with a Betalight in the top of a normal waggler. At just 3–4yd range the floats stood out like beacons and the bites were tremendously positive. The floats would simply sway, drift a few inches and disappear into the murky water. Each night, the pair caught ten or a dozen fish within an hour or two, and had permission been granted to fish for longer then 100lb bags would probably have been on the cards.

THE FLOAT-LEDGER METHOD

Many of the older angling books recommended this method for fishing stillwaters, primarily at some range where the swims were generally between 3ft and 8ft deep. The thinking was that the float gave a better bite indication than any other and so could be used successfully in conjunction with the lead.

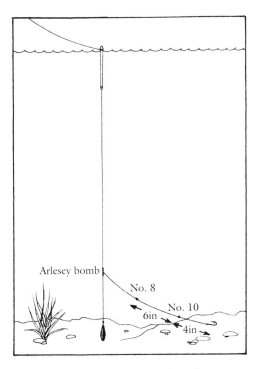

Fig. 18 A float-ledgering rig for still waters.

By and large, however, new and improved ledgering techniques and bite indications have rendered the float-ledger method pretty well obsolete. Ledgering today is such an art form that the skilled practitioner can detect a pectoral waving at a maggot from 50yd. In fact, I have only had occasion to use the float-ledger method twice in the past ten years.

Perhaps the most effective occasion was on a large, shallow estate lake where the bottom was covered thickly in a green algae, something that is very common these days since lakes have become overenriched with nutrients. However, here and there the algae had been scraped away in well-known feeding places where the bream and tench made a habit of stopping off to forage. If a bait could be put into these small, clear areas (often no larger than a fishing-basket top) then action could be expected. Passing fish were likely to investigate the area and a bait was bound to be taken.

The problem with traditional ledgering on this lake was that I was never quite sure whether my bait had landed in exactly the right spot. It only needed to be a couple of inches out and the bait would lie quite uselessly under the green carpet. The float-ledger method did, however, allow me to place the bait absolutely accurately and obviously I had a visual confirmation of this.

The float that served me best on this occasion was a windbeater – that is, a waggler with both a body and a sight bob. The body allowed me to get away with a waggler that was not too great in length – as the swim was shallow and the water was clear, neither bream nor tench would put up with a long waggler in these little pockets. The sight bob was also useful as some of the pockets of weed-free water were anything up to 40–50yd from the bank. At such ranges a straight waggler, never mind an insert, becomes very difficult to see after some while.

The line, of course, was sunk quite deeply right the way to the rod and the whole set-up was surprisingly stable even in quite high winds. The lead could be substituted with either an open-ended or a closed swimfeeder, and indeed this proved to be the most efficient type of weight as a tight clustering of loose feed could be placed in exactly the right area just underneath the float. Catapulting, especially in anything like a wind, tended to spray at least some of the loose feed into useless, weed-covered oblivion.

In practice, the method was exciting one. The water was so clear that in anything like sunny conditions the shoals of bream and tench could be seen moving around. As soon as fish began to drift over the area of sand beneath the float, expectancy rose high level. Often it was possible to see the fish tip up, and even to see the small puffs of silt that they disturbed. Bites tended to be dramatically sudden: one instant the sight bob would be riding there and then would be totally buried within the bat of an eyelid.

I cannot say that huge catches were taken using this method but I found that it was a very useful one to use in the highly specialized conditions.

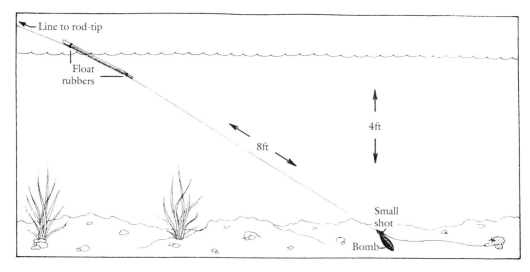

Fig. 19 Float-ledger rig.

The second application of the float-ledger method I found was when fishing the clear River Wensum for barbel. In this particular swim accurate placing of the bait was again essential. The bait had to be put in one or two of the small depressions where the barbel fed regularly. These were about 2–3ft long and often only about 8–9in wide. Chub tended to feed quite generally around the area, but the barbel virtually always made for these small depressions that they had created themselves in their constant grubbing for food.

The problem was that the barbel were very quick to accept and then eject a bait. Hair and bolt rigs might have sorted this out, but my approach at the time was to watch the bait and strike as immediately as I could. However, watching a couple of grains of corn over quite long periods proved to very tiring and frequently I found I was watching a free offering by mistake! If a float was put up the line, this gave me a very good sighting and tended to confirm almost at once which bait on the bottom was in actual fact attached to a hook. Also, it was possible to watch the float itself and not the headache-inducing bait: bites were signalled immediately on the float which simply vanished in an instant.

The method worked very well at comparatively short distances – ideally between two and three rod lengths out. The idea was to use quite a large stick float, the line from it to the rod tip being kept clear of the water entirely. By keeping the rod tip well up in the air no line at all fell on the water and the waggler itself lay flat. Bites simply pulled the float straight under, so fast that it barely seemed to cock! The rod, of course, was propped up on a rest during these long periods and my hand lay continually on the butt, ready for an immediate strike.

It is surprising how many times this method worked. The strike could be made before the barbel ejected the bait, and because every-thing was so instant pressure could be piled on immediately before the barbel could make it to the nearby snags and sanctuary. The method was an exciting and often an efficient one, though it was made very difficult by a strong downstream wind or during periods of weed cutting when floating rubbish tended to clog the float and make the whole thing very frustrating.

THE 'LIFT' METHOD

The 'lift' method is another very old technique that came back into common usage in the 1950s after being publicized by F. J. Taylor and his immediate circle. Sadly, during the last few years the method seems to have drifted back, wrongly, into relative obscurity. The Taylor brothers, as they were called, reinvented the method specifically for tench when they were fishing from the punt on Wootton Lake, and they had tremendous success with it.

The method uses a length of peacock quill attached by the bottom only. The shot is placed approximately 1in from the hook. The idea is that you set the float so that you are fishing 4–6in deeper than the actual depth, although this can be more if there is a wind and sub-surface currents. After casting you draw the tackle tight; a rod rest is essential here for you cannot hold the rod steady enough for long enough. Bites are registered by the float lifting and falling flat, and as soon as this happens you strike. This is a deadly tench method, especially when using smaller baits like maggot, caster and corn, although it does work well with breadflake.

It is a mistake to think that the method is only good for tench: roach, carp and bream all respond well to it. Also, if the method is used in a very light, scaled-down form it can prove deadly for the crucian carp.

The happiness of a float-caught carp.

Obviously, the method is somewhat limited in its uses – especially as it can only really be fished close to the margins and because a very strong wind, for example, does upset its efficiency. Once again, a long, sensitive rod is of great benefit and the old length of peacock quill is hard to beat.

THE FAST-WATER AVON-TYPE FLOAT METHOD

Freelining used to be one of my favourite methods, and it is a comparatively simple one that can be mastered with only a little experience. It pays to put on thigh boots and stand in the middle of the river at the head of turbulent water. There is nothing on the line apart from the hook and a large bait which you allow to swim freely down the rapids beneath you. Try to keep a constant check on the bait as it goes, for a fish can be deep-hooked. This, in fact, is the key to freelining: the ability to keep in constant touch with the bait through water, however rough it may be. Bites can be very vigorous and you often feel them right down the rod to your left hand which is holding the line; when you do so, strike at once. Freelining is an excellent method for bold-biting fish like chub with big baits such as flake and lobworm, but it is not particularly flexible for smaller, shyer fish or less hectically feeding species. This is where the Avon float comes in.

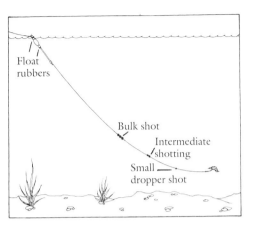

Fig. 20 A basic Avon rig.

The ideal swim for the Avon is the same type as mentioned above, probably where the water is bubbling through a weir or down some rapids and the fish you are after are chub or occasionally roach, barbel and dace. Areas like this are particularly favoured in the early part of the season as both barbel and chub seem to seek out fast, well-oxygenated water after spawning. It might have something to do with cleaning themselves as angling folk-lore has it, but this I personally doubt. My opinion is that it has something to do with the food stocks, for at this time of the year the fast, gravelly shallows team with small fry, minnows and insect larvae.

The Avon float allows you to fish in very much a freelining type of way, but offers more control and better bite indication. Also, you are not tied to large baits but can use maggots, casters and grains of sweetcorn. This type of float fishing is hard work and generally you will be through the swim in half a minute or so, so the action is pretty constant.

A perfect trotting swim.

Generally, the float is best set so that the bait swims a little below mid-water. This obviously can vary, and if barbel are being sought then you need to put the bait as near to the bottom as possible – not easy in water as fast as this. This is a situation when heavy feeding can pay dividends, especially when you are pretty sure that there are several fish in front of you and the water is warm enough to provoke them into feeding ravenously. In fact, I often feed a handful of corn or maggots at virtually every cast, getting chub in particular boiling on the surface or glinting just a few inches beneath. Even when this happens it is a good idea to fish the bait around mid-water, for the larger fish often hang a little below the rest of the shoal members.

Bites are invariably dramatic . . . at least, at first until the shoal begins to wise up after the initial casualties. It can then be time for a different bait: why not try a dead minnow? These are after all probably the most natural of baits in such circumstances and could be exactly what that big five-pounder down there is looking for.

Do not, under any circumstances, keep chub or barbel in keepnets at this time of the year when they have just spawned. It is all too tempting to build up a big weight of fish and display it to the camera at the end of the day. However, just think of the stress and trauma such an action has on a fish which is recovering from the rigours of its spawning period. Indeed, outside match fishing it is hard to think of any occasion where a keepnet is useful or desirable for the lone pleasure or specialist angler. Leave them at home.

THE LONG-TROTTING METHOD

Long-trotting is the term given to fishing the float downriver quite long distances – certainly over 15yd and often up to almost 100yd! Yes,

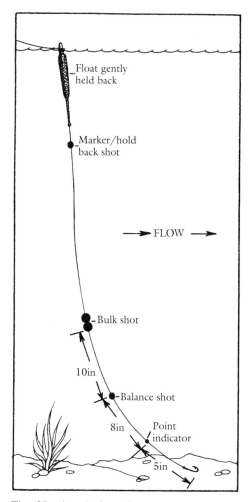

Fig. 21 A typical trotting set-up.

100yd – a distance possible for the eagle-eyed. Even for the less physically gifted, distances of 70–80yd are quite possible.

Long-trotting has certain obvious advantages. First, it is an ideal way of finding fish in a fairly featureless stretch of river. If there is no response after the first dozen or so casts, then it is quite in order to move down 70–80yd (if space permits) and fish the next stretch of river. By travelling light and frequently, even a mile of river can be fished

This chub was caught at a range of 60yd.

quite thoroughly within a morning. This style of fishing is very useful for featureless rivers where the head of fish is not particularly high.

The second major use of long-trotting is to contact fish that are very shy and will not tolerate close human proximity. Very frequently rivers like this are fast, clear and shallow where species such as chub, grayling or roach are particularly easily spooked.

As usual, a long rod is very useful, combined with excellent reel control whether this be centre-pin or fixed spool. The arts demanded are many: the line must be mended continually so that control of the float is constant; and the float has to be guided towards promising areas, inched around snags, held up occasionally so that the bait rises enticingly, or allowed to go with the full flow of the current.

When the float does eventually go at long distances the strike needs to be instant and powerful, and must continue until the pull of a hooked fish is felt. Everything has to be gentle, confident and with a smooth power. Hitting a fish, especially a large one, at 80–90yd in a swift current can be quite a shock on tackle and angler alike. First of all, there is the test of the tackle. The line must be of the right strength and must be flawless; equally, the hook must be chosen with great care.

After the fish is hooked, keep the rod low to avoid splashing the fish on the surface – such activity will only alarm the rest of the shoal and make a hook-slip more likely. With, say, a chub, there is likely to be ten or fifteen seconds of stalemate between angler and fish before the latter begins to give ground. Once the fish begins to come, keep it on the move with a steady, horizontal pumping action. Pull the fish 3–4yd and then reel line in quickly, repeating the process as necessary. Keep that rod low all the time, and with luck the fish will continue to fight beneath the surface.

Ideal conditions for long-trotting in my book are dull, overcast days when there is little wind to ruffle the surface. Bright sunlight leads to a lot of surface glare, which in turn makes seeing the float a long way off a headache-inducing job. Wind chop on the river is at least as bad, especially when combined with glinting sunlight. A wind of any strength, especially across the stream, makes float control at long ranges even more difficult than it is normally. All this does not mean to say that long-trotting in breezy, bright conditions is impossible, but it does perhaps pay to build up experience on the calmer, dull days when fish are more inclined to bite anyway. With luck, on such days you will even see fish (especially roach or chub or dace) top on the surface, and this sight can only serve to build up confidence.

Loose feeding is a problem at long range and probably the best bet is to feed in dribbles of mashed bread, possibly flavoured and possibly containing maggots, casters or even pieces of chopped worm. This concoction will gradually drift down the river, hopefully bringing the fish on the feed or even pulling them closer up to the angler. If the hookbait is a fairly large piece of flake then loose feed is not all that important. However, with maggots this is not the case, and a shoal of roach will generally need to see quite a few loose offerings before they start really turning on to the feed.

If fish have been located at 70yd or even 80yd and you do not think there is a great deal of chance that you will spook them, then by all means move down closer to them. Long-trotting can be used simply as a way of finding fish and, once located, you can move in on them and fish in a more tight, delicate way. Certainly, I never really like playing a 2lb-plus roach at long range on light tackle with a size 16 or 18 hook being the only thing connecting us. I can remember that during fight after fight my heart was in my mouth absolutely every second of the fish's course to the net.

The Dorset Stour – a perfect float water for roach.

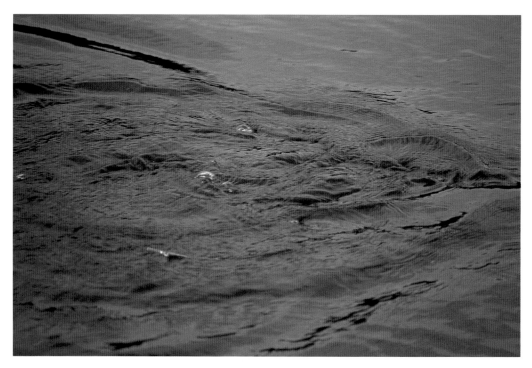

The float eventually breaks surface.

A Scottish pike boils under the float.

The old quill float rides above the bubbles.

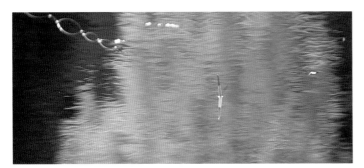

A close-up of a peacock quill.

Carp float and chick in a
frame.

A large pike that fell to a float-fished deadbait.

A big perch that fell to float-fished livebait.

The author crouches with a big crucian that is about to be landed.

An immaculate roach caught on double maggot under the float.

Back goes a float-caught barbel.

A nice float-caught bream.

A superb Scottish pike that fell to a float paternostered bait rig.

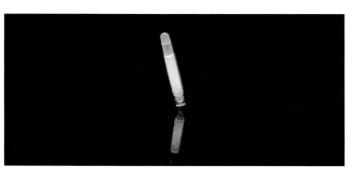

The night float stands out like a beacon.

Drifter floats bob in the distance.

Blickling Lake – a perfect float water for bream and tench.

6 Float Fishing for Roach

FLOATS FOR STILLWATER ROACH

In a strange sort of way success can be detrimental in that it breeds a certain smugness and a reluctance to change a winning method, even when that method is no longer drawing fish! Over the years, I have had a good number of big roach and this is a species with which I feel entirely comfortable . . . and with which I am probably very blinkered indeed! One time when I did change my methods with success all started when I heard about a lake with some very big fish in it and set about immediate investigation.

The 'method' was quite obvious. I chose to ledger some 100yd up from the dam where the lake broadened out and also opened out. The trees grew in abundance from this point and warm, gentle westerlies generally gave the surface a good ripple. My approach was to groundbait with bread, corn and casters halfway across, and ledger two baits into the area. I was not sure how many big roach there were in the lake, but I was quite convinced that sooner or later they would bump into me and I would catch fish.

Well, it did not actually happen like that. In around half a dozen trips I had three decent bites, one of which I rolled and two of which I missed. I was tempted to put this down to the large number of very small roach in the lake that were probably nibbling at my baits without giving any decisive indication. This was a convenient answer and I never really considered any other. Now, I am not so sure.

Anyway, on the sixth evening I packed up and walked along the lake, through the trees and towards the dam. As I passed, a large fish rolled some 3–4yd out. I stopped to watch and within the next ten minutes another four very heavy roach showed in the half-light. Not unnaturally, I was back the next day, using the same technique but closer to the dam in the deeper water that I found there. Again, I had no real indications on the bobbin, but again casters were sucked and this time maggots had been chewed. I could not be sure, but I felt small fish were responsible. Then another nice roach rolled and I began to worry. I do not really like to change from the ledgered approach when after big roach and I could see no reason why they should be shy of it, but still I turned to the float.

I was fishing at a range of only 4yd so I chose a very light link waggler that carried five number 4 shot. The water was calm and the only undertow was a slight pull towards the dam. Although I was 20yd from the dam this flow was just enough to make presentation a little tricky on such light, tight gear. I did, however, have one tentative bite and struck for a split second into what seemed like a good fish. However, I was not happy at all. Then, in quick succession, two big fish rolled 10yd to my left very close to the outfall.

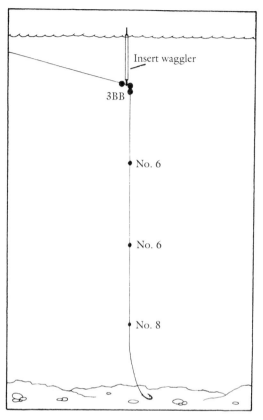

Fig. 22 A simple waggler set-up for a still water.

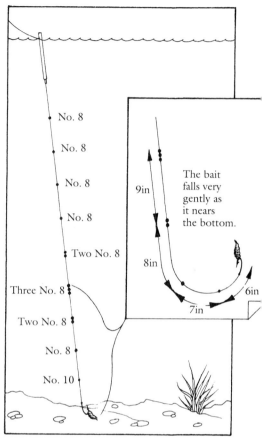

Fig. 23 A stick float set-up for still waters.

I crept along the bank to investigate. Visibility was around 12in and I noticed when I threw in maggots that there was a definite flow – indeed, it was just as fast as on the Bure or the Wensum.

This called for something of a rethink and I changed the float ring to a small stick float fished, obviously, double rubber. I sat some 60yd from the dam and began to fish the swim just as I would on a slow-moving river. After about twenty minutes I was holding the float back 2yd or even less from the dam, imagining the bait just lifting fractionally in the water. Then there was no float there and the force of the take pulled the rod tip round

before I could strike! That roach was not the biggest that I have ever caught, nor was it anywhere near the largest ir the lake, but at just over 1½lb it was a more than welcome sight. I do not say that I went on to decimate those fish during the course of the day, but I picked up another couple of good fish and the whole process of catching them on the float appealed to me greatly.

LAYING-ON IN RIVERS

I was introduced to laying-on in rivers as a child by one of the best anglers I have ever known. On the River Dane in Cheshire he absolutely slaughtered the roach from right under his rod tip when I myself struggled with all possible methods.

What I learnt then as a child is that laying-on is the most delicate, sensitive method of catching shy river fish, especially roach. There are several important things to bear in mind: first, the amount the float is fished overdepth depends largely on the speed of the current – the faster the current, the more the float has to be fished overdepth; second, the float must be fished top and bottom for obvious reasons of control; and third, it is futile to lay on in rivers at too long a distance – ideally, the float should be very close to the rod tip.

A long rod is a boon with this method as it gives more control further away from the bank. Personally, I cannot find any modern-built float to beat the old, traditional quill as a suitable material. There is something about the shape, adaptable size and buoyancy of a quill that makes it ideal. Reels are a matter of choice, and those that can use centre-pins generally swear by them. Line strengths, hook size and bait are obviously related to the fish that are being sought.

There are also a few wrinkles to the method, the first being that bites are often quick and positive, and pressure from the rod tip will be felt by the fish if an instant strike is not made. For this reason, support the rod on a rest by all means, but at the same time hold the butt ready for action. Also, ensure that the loose feed is kept very tight around the area indeed. If it breaks up and floats off downriver all you are doing is spreading the fish out and reducing your own chances accordingly. A bait-dropper is a very useful tool for this type of fishing.

A big fish that fell for delicate bait presentation.

It is fair to say that most of my big float-caught roach have been taken while laying-on. There is something about the method that makes it absolutely ideal for cautious, big fish. Obviously, the fact that the float is close means that it is quite easy to see at dawn and dusk – both killing times. In hours of true darkness it is also quite possible to insert a Betalight into the top of a piece of quill and either whip or superglue it there.

Ideally, I like the float to be cocked at around forty-five degrees. Sometimes it is good to have it lying flat, but generally I like it at an angle as bites can be indicated either by the float rising or lying quite flat. Sometimes it moves upstream or downstream, and sometimes is gone within the twinkling of an eye. Strike quickly at anything that is obviously positive. If the fish are particularly fast-biting then it can pay to put a fairly large shot 3–4ft up the line from the float towards the rod tip. This gives just a little bit of slack line – only a few inches – which in its turn adds a half-second or so to the strike time.

Choice of swim is obviously vital and the method cannot be used on very shallow or very quick water. The slower, deeper eddy is ideal and the float will sit happily just on the crease or just out into the main flow. A gentle flow can be coped with and the water certainly does not have to be totally slack. These types of current are favoured by the roach anyway, and very little is being missed in ordinary circumstances if this method is used.

STRET PEGGING

Stret pegging is a method as old as Izaak himself and yet is very little used on today's rivers. This is a great pity because it is extremely efficient method for roach, dace, chub and barbel – and even bream where they are present.

The method is rather like laying-on but on a rather larger scale. The idea is that a fairly large float is fished top and bottom and overdepth. The difference between stretpegging and laying-on is that with the former method the float can be trundled slowly and carefully around the swim rather than being stationary in one area of it. Stret pegging takes a fair amount of practice before it can be used absolutely efficiently. The key is to use a long rod and not to be too ambitious to start with.

The ideal swim is a large eddy of fairly gentle pace around 4–8ft deep. The idea is to fish

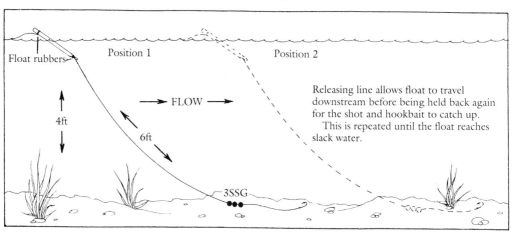

Fig. 24 Stret-pegging rig.

the float quite a way overdepth (again this depends on the water speed and the depth of the swim), and to let the current push the float slowly around the swim, searching for fish as it goes. The float is fished top and bottom, the rod has to be held high and contact maintained with the float at all times. When the float stops, allow it thirty seconds to a minute and then lift it and ease it on its way again. Bites tend to be very positive and quite distinguishable from the bait simply dragging on the bottom and pulling the float under.

Once a bit of expertise has been won on the slacks, it is possible to fish the method in the main flow – providing this is not too savage. The same technique applies: you simply fish a high rod and keep the line tight to the float so that it is always on the surface unless pulled under by a taking fish. You can begin by fishing the float right under the rod tip and then allowing the current to ease it gently away from you. In this way you can comb a 10–15yd stretch of water at a very slow rate indeed. Thus, stret pegging has all the advantages of using, say, a stick float, yet it allows you to fish through the swim much more slowly. The method, therefore, is especially useful for big, wary fish that often take some time in making up their minds.

A large quill float is ideal for the job, but an Avon-type float will also work well, its size dependent on the depth and speed of the water to be fished. Baits are commonly maggots or casters, but breadflake also works well. Feed is simply dribbled into the head of the swim or a little above so that it hits the bottom and travels slowly down the stream.

Stret pegging is definitely a method for the later months of the season once the frosts and floods have cleared off the weed and as much bottom debris as possible. In fact, a relatively clean bottom is almost essential if the method is to work properly – and when it does work properly, it is an absolute killer.

STICK-FLOAT FISHING ON EASTERN RIVERS

The typical swim that I have in mind for this method is around 4–6ft deep on a very slow moving, comparatively narrow river such as the Wensum, Waveney, Upper Yare or Gipping. There are many such rivers throughout lowland England, especially in the flat eastern counties. The species hunted will be predominantly roach with the odd chub, dace or even stray barbel. The flow on such a river is so slow that if there is an upstream wind the float hardly seems to move at all . . . but it does and very often the delicate stick float is the best way to take roach, especially during the day. The bait will probably be maggots or caster and the roach will generally be between 1lb and even 3lb in weight, very shy and very careful about what they do.

The actual float control here is not difficult at all, for the water is barely moving and it is unlikely that you have to fish at lengths much exceeding 10–15yd. In fact, it will often take five to six minutes to fish out such a length, even when hardly holding the float back at all.

The key to this type of fishing is sensitive feeding: feed too many maggots and the roach simply turn off; feed too few maggots and they will never really begin in the first place. This is a method for the winter months, especially after Christmas when the water can be low, clear and cold and all weed growth has disappeared. At times like these the roach are especially finicky. One way to land them is by ledgering lumps of bread in known roach holes at night, but not everybody wants to do this – hardly surprising when one considers how cold and boring such nights can be!

Wind conditions are not too critical for this close-in style of fishing, though a strong downstream wind can hurry the bait through rather faster than you would like and equally a strong upstream wind will stop the bait

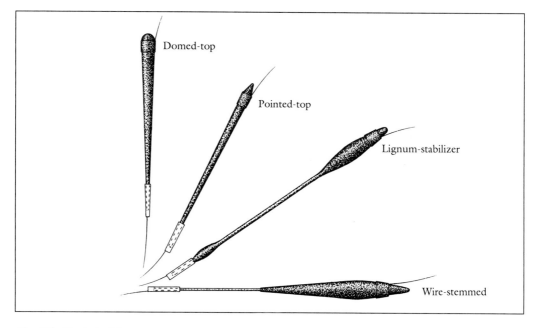

Fig. 25 Typical sticks.

altogether. Light conditions are very important. Generally, bright light and clear, cold water are the kiss of death to this type of fishing and only the after-dark approach is possible, *but* there are exceptions. I have known times when for no apparent reason, midday, when the sun is at its highest, has brought on a totally unexpected feeding spell and several big fish have fallen by the early afternoon.

Bites are usually unmistakable and even the normal shy-biting roach will move the float in no uncertain terms. Generally the float disappears, but sometimes it will shimmy either to the left, right, upstream or downstream before disappearing. At such close range the strike should always be met with resistance.

The perfect swim is hard to define and many unexpected ones have given sport on certain occasions. On a river like the Wensum there are certain long-standing roach swims, but often a shoal will move elsewhere for a short while. It is perfect if you see fish prime on the surface in the early morning or the late evening and can form an accurate position of their whereabouts, but this is ever more rare these days. Obvious swims to look for are deeper bends; the crease on the outside of eddies; slow, deep runs past any fallen trees or noticeable snags; and especially those areas alongside decaying cabbage patches where the bottom consists of quite clean sand or gravel. A stretch of water under overhanging alders is often a favourite as are those runs close to dense reedbeds. The areas just up and downstream of bridges are also worth investigating, but then some totally characterless stretches of river have often held roach in great numbers for long periods in the past, so do not rule out any yard of the river entirely.

The stick float can present some exciting possibilities. In my book *Roach – The Gentle Giants* (The Crowood Press, 1987) there is a photograph of a very young John Bailey opposite page 96 holding a large roach. The

A roach that was taken on the stick float with the bait held back.

A glorious big roach.

caption reads: 'John Bailey holding a summer-caught two-pound roach, taken on the trot.' This is, however, rather a bald statement and could do with some addition of how I edged and teased it down the swim.

Now, I knew that a shoal of big fish were resident in the run. The problem was that they would not take a bait anchored on the bottom, only a moving one and only one that really tantalized them.

I still recall that morning with great excitement. I would edge the float down towards the fish with a large piece of flake trundling 3–4ft beneath it. Mostly the roach would drift out of the way of the flake, but if I kept holding the float back so that the flake rose and fell in the water, fish would come to investigate. By holding the float back yet again I could dibble it virtually on the nose of a curious roach. This was the taking time; it was as though they became mesmerized with the dancing, rising and falling flake, and after a

few seconds of having the bait in their mouth this would go.

I have little doubt that using the quill like a stick float was the only tool that would have caught me that particular fish and several others that morning before the shoal broke up and dispersed. The method was thrilling highly effective.

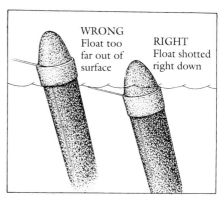

Fig. 26 How to shot the stick float.

7   *Float Fishing for Pike and Perch*

Thankfully, the days of the Fishing Gazette bung are way behind us. These cork creations were the pike floats of my youth and pretty useless they were too. The concept was that the line ran through the middle where it was stopped at the required point by a peg. Many anglers used the bung in conjunction with a pilot float – a smaller, round cork float placed a yard or two up the line. The horrifying concept behind this was that once the bung was pulled under the angler could wait for a few minutes while the pike swallowed the bait, and by watching the pilot float would have some idea where the fish had gone. The strike thereafter hardly needed to be crisp and clean – the angler merely had to reel in, decapitate the pike and retrieve his hook from the gullet!

A superb big pike.

The day of the pilot float and the bung began to slip into its sorry sunset in the 1960s, and now such atrocities are hardly ever seen on the bank. One of many bad things about the bung was the fact that it was impossible to strike cleanly through it. Very often the whole water erupted as the bung sprang out on the strike, and unless the pike was deep-hooked, it would probably eject the bait at this point. The modern pike floats generally, if not always, run freely up and down the line so that the problem of water displacement does not really exist.

Virtually all pike floats today are made from moulded plastics. This material is totally waterproof and therefore does not sink lower and lower throughout the course of the day. It is also resistant to the grooving effect of lines and is very buoyant for its weight. There are three major shapes in use. The first is a long, pencil-shaped float – the Drennan piker is the perfect example. The concept is that this is the perfect deadbait float: it offers little resistance to a taking pike and, being long, shows very easily at distance. This might not

necessarily catch more pike, but it is obviously a very valuable conservation aid. If you cannot see the float clearly, it is often difficult to decide when to strike, and the piker is certainly a big and obvious float. A deep-hooked pike cannot really be blamed now on the float but rather on the angler.

In high winds, surface tow can be just as big a problem for the pike angler as it is for the roach or bream fisherman. For this reason Drennan has brought out the pike waggler float. The principle is pretty much the same as with any normal float. It is attached by its bottom end only – either by a link swivel or by pushing the line direct through the float eye. In this way, the line between the rod tip and the float can be sunk and therefore the float has to combat considerably less drift. There is nothing more annoying than a float being pulled under – as can often happen at range on a windy day. Again, the development of the pike waggler float is a major conservation development and should be adopted by any considerate angler.

There remains the third major shape of pike floats now commonly on the market. These are shorter, more dumpy floats like the zeppler. The idea here is that they are more buoyant and more resistant, therefore making the ideal livebait float. Remember, a livebait float must not be pulled consistently under by the bait working against it. If this happens, it is virtually impossible to decipher whether a pike has actually taken the bait or whether the bait is simply being lively. The tendency is to ignore the dipping float and to end up with a deep-hooked pike. You should therefore always go for the squatter float when livebaiting.

Again, with conservation in mind do make sure that your float is coloured properly for the day and the water conditions. Most floats now come in a bright neon-orange which is highly visible, but if for some reason it is not

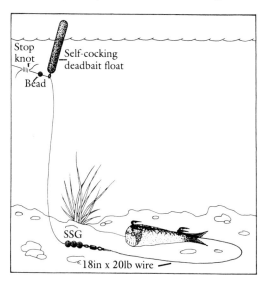

Fig. 27 Deadbait rig.

then take appropriate action. Remember: a delayed strike is a dead pike.

Virtually all modern floats are now stopped on the line by either a ledger stop or a slider knot. A ledger stop is fine if the swim you are fishing is not too deep – certainly shallower than three-quarters of the length of the rod. Anything above that and casting a large bait becomes a nightmare. (Indeed, fifty per cent depth is far more desirable.) If the swim is a deep one, obviously the slider knot tied with either very thick nylon or power gum is the obvious choice. Remember that there is a great deal of pressure on the slider knot when pike fishing, and the weights and distances involved can often dislodge a single slider knot. A double slider knot, however, is pretty well immovable and will stand up to the rigours of the most demanding cast. Do not let the ends of the slider knot dangle too long or they will not flow through the rod eyes properly. Cut them to as short a length as possible and they will fly through.

I shall now look at certain areas where the use of a float is really advisable in pike fishing.

THE DRIFTER FLOAT

It has long been a preoccupation of pike anglers to get baits a long way from their bank, especially when a boat is not available. On large waters pike can be anywhere, especially near snags or other features dotted around the water, and the man whose casting ability is limited is obviously going to miss out on these far-flung fish. The other question is one of pressure: on heavily fished waters pike tend to drift out of reach of the ordinary angler and a lot of bankside activity will gradually force packs of pike way out into the middle. Long casting with specially adapted tackle is one way to combat this. However, it does have its own problems: a cast of 80–100yd

will generally kill all but the toughest livebait; and fish lying between the bank and this distance remain completely uncovered. Very often a long-distance bait is merely propelled way over the pikes' heads.

The answer to this dilemma is frequently to use the drifter float. The drifter float was pioneered many years ago by that inventive pike man Eddie Turner. Eddie's list of big pike is amazing and a major reason for this is his inventiveness as well as his dedication. Nowhere is his forward thinking better shown than in the development of the drifter float. The drifter float design has come a long way since the early days and now there are several different varieties on the market. The concept of them all is the same: using the wind to catch a large-vaned float, the piker can drift his bait vast distances out over the water in front of him. In fact, it is possible to control a bait effectively at 200yd or at times, even a little more.

Obviously, the rod must be long and powerful if the line is to be mended and a decent strike is to be put in on a taking fish at such range – 12ft 2½–3lb test curve rods are actually about ideal. The reel must also be a big one, for over 200yd of 11–15lb line must be stored on its spool. It is obviously an advantage if the spool can also be metal as sometimes plastic can shatter under the enormous pressure of a long retrieve with a big fish on the end. The shattered spool will merely cause tangles and lost fish. The line itself should be of the toughest and most abrasion-resistant type. Also, lines with little stretch are a boon when it comes to striking into a pike at anything over 100yd.

So, what is the technique? The diagram (*see* Fig. 28) shows the rig exactly. The important thing is to have wind which ideally should be force 2 to 4; once it begins to gust above force 5 than problems do start. Begin with the wind behind you, cast the rig some 10–15yd to

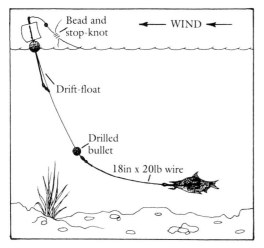

Fig. 28 Drift-float set-up.

where the ripples start and begin to pay out line. Start greasing the line at once. There are gadgets available for this job – you simply pack them with grease and insert them into one of the rod rings. However, over the years, I've found that a bit of rag smeared liberally with line grease and pushed into the bottom ring is just as efficient. Also, the rag is easily removed when casting is called for. Do not neglect the use of line grease for it is imperative that the line floats from rod tip to float, even (or especially) at a range of 200yd. If the line sinks the float does not travel out properly, it is impossible to guide it and, even worse, a strike is frequently made ineffective.

As the float begins to move away from the bank, being driven by the wind, it pays to check it frequently and stop the line peeling from the spool. When this happens, the float moves either to the right or left over quite a large arc and therefore covers a great deal more water and, possibly, more pike. I tend to stop the float every 5–10yd and therefore work a very large area out into the lake or pit.

Once the float is more than 70yd or so from the bank it is really vital to keep an eye on it

all the time. A taking pike does not always pull it under the surface; sometimes there is a quick move to the right or left, or the float lies flat. Binoculars are a great aid to bite detection and it is important to have the right coloured vane to suit the conditions on the day. Orange is a consistent favourite. It is vital to see the bite early for you have to wind down, often mend a big bow in the line and then strike over a long distance before setting the hooks. If there is any delay in this a deep-hooked pike is a probability – something none of us wants in this enlightened day and age.

A word about striking: the drifter float strike technique is not a strike in the normal sense of the word. Rather, you wind down until everything is tight and then walk backwards with the rod at an angle of forty-five degrees. The bend in it grows and grows, and at last when nothing more will give it pays to give a bit of a heave. The hooks should now be well and truly set. Playing a fish at immense distances is also an exhilarating, exciting and often problematic affair. At long ranges the pike is inclined to kite – that is when the momentum of the fish works with the pull of the rod to swing the fish off course and pretty much out of control. A possible solution that works in some circumstances is to relax the pressure altogether so that the fish can find its own course again. Many other problems are also associated with playing fish at such long range: dying weedbeds, unknown gravel bars, sunken and abandoned machinery, fallen tree branches from long eroded islands and a multitude of other potential hazards exist. For this reason it is always useful to have a boat available in case of emergencies. It is never tolerable to leave a fish in a snag if anything can be done to prevent it. After playing a fish in from a long distance always check the line to make sure that there are no abrasions or weaknesses that could cause a snap-off in the future.

The size of bait is an important consideration when using the drifter. If it is too large it will affect the progress of the float, and it might prove difficult to set the hooks from a large bait into a pike's mouth at extreme distance. On the other hand, a small bait is often less likely to arouse a pike's interest if it is moving over the pike at quite a speed. The answer is to go for a medium sized bait of around 4–6oz. Livebaits are the norm, but deadbaits can also work very well on occasion, mounted head-down and allowed to trundle over the bars and likely looking drop-offs. Setting the hooks is always a problem at such long range, and if abortive strikes are being made then it is as well to consider the use of a flying hook which is positioned outside of the bait.

Drifter Problems

I have written about the capture of a 36lb pike on the drifter float rig before, so I will not bore readers of this present book with the same tale . . . except to say that when I hit into the fish at around 125–150yd it was one of the most thrilling moments of my life and an experience I wouldn't trade for any other.

No, the tale that I want to tell now concerns the same lake, the Norfolk Flyfishers, but relates to a much smaller fish – in fact one that was exactly half the size. On the Monday a good wind was blowing from the club house bank and Dan Leary caught a whole legion of fish from there. I was siting about a quarter of a mile away and every time I saw his rod bend

A 36lb pike that fell to the drifting method.

The result of a float-fished livebait.

I felt that this could be yet another big fish. However, it was not to be and most of them weighed 10–20lb. Not surprisingly, the next day I took Dan's vacant swim and began to fish it with a couple of drift floats. After their hammering the previous day, the fish had obviously moved further from the bank and I was picking them up at around 80–100yd.

Just after midday the float dived and I was into what felt like a very good fish, but only for a few seconds before it snagged irretrievably. I tried every trick I knew to free the fish, but to no avail. Fortunately, however, a boat was moored close by. I was rowed to where the fish was stuck fast, and in the clear water I could see it tethered firmly round an old piece of discarded nylon. It was quite an easy matter to scoop the fish into the boat where it could be unhooked and returned quickly. There is no doubt that had the boat not been available that fish would have suffered greatly and would probably even have died, tethered immovably 100yd from the bank. The moral is simple: whenever possible arrange access to a boat when using this very satisfying and effective method.

THE FLOAT PATERNOSTER RIG

The diagram (*see* Fig. 29) makes it clear that knowledge of the depth is imperative for this method – accurate plumbing is essential before setting the stop knot. There is little that is difficult about the rig, its main use being to tether a livebait close to a known ambush area or snag. The bait does not have to roam in order to entice a pike from cover and, in fact, the ideal is to place the rig as close as possible to a fish – sometimes one that can even be seen.

It is very common these days to see livebaits being fished on the sunken float rig with bite indicators used to indicate a take. Obviously,

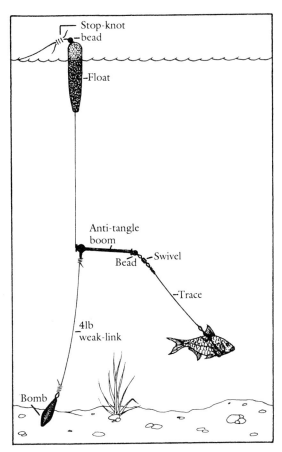

Fig. 29 Float Paternoster rig.

this method works and great numbers of fish have been caught over the years, but I still maintain that a more instant type of indication can be achieved by using a surface float. There are few occasions that the float paternoster rig is not applicable and, when using it, a take is immediately obvious.

A Take on the Float Paternoster

As with the last account, I was again at the Flyfishers but this time the fish was enormous. Roger Miller and I were fishing the renowned Pontoon Swim where a deep channel runs along the bank and turns a corner to

This fish fell to a float at night whilst the torch was played upon the water.

a bay. Over the years many fish have fallen from this area and we were reasonably confident of something in the coming week. Most of the people around us elected to use sunken float rigs but we, as usual, opted for the float paternoster.

At about midday strange things began to happen to those floats. There were sudden bursts of activity when one, two or even all four would jig madly up and down, shoot sideways and even occasionally bob under for an instant. We did not get a proper take and neither was the bait actually marked, but we felt sure that something was happening down there. I doubt now whether there would have been any real indication at the butt end of things and, had we not had floats, we might well not have been as alert as we were.

These spasms of excitement came in odd, concentrated bursts, each lasting about ten or fifteen minutes. A lull would follow and then the floats would once again become agitated. Nobody around us was really aware of the tension that we felt, but we were quite sure that a fish or even a group of fish was passing backwards and forwards through the swim. We were also quite sure that once the light levels fell sufficiently whatever was responsible would make up its mind and feed in earnest.

We were proved correct. A float dipped and Roger Miller struck. The rest became history. What I will never forget is his upturned face, glowing in triumph as he straddled a pike only a handful of ounces under 40lb.

Of course, it could be said that the fish would have fallen to a sunken float rig. This is very probably true, but then again, without the indication on the visible floats, who knows? If we had used a sunken float rig perhaps we would have thought the swim dead and moved to another spot, leaving this big fish to somebody else or even to swim completely free.

THE ROVING LIVEBAIT RIG

Again, the diagram (*see* Fig. 30) really explains how the float is used in this instance. The line should be greased to allow better control of the float and also to cut down the amount of weight that the livebait has to tow behind it. The main purpose of using the float for this rig is to suspend the bait so that it is free to travel large distances and, hopefully, to cover more hungry pike.

This is an excellent rig to use when the water is clear and deadbait do not seem to work very efficiently. It is also an excellent rig on little-known waters as a great area is covered when possible pike lies are narrowed down.

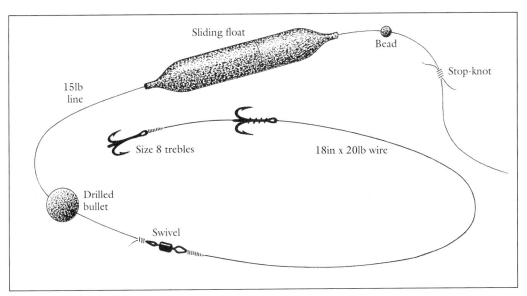

Sliding float

Bead

Stop-knot

15lb line

Size 8 trebles

18in x 20lb wire

Drilled bullet

Swivel

Fig. 30 Roving livebait rig.

An Early Eleven-Pounder

The year was 1972 and the water was Selbrigg Pond in north Norfolk. My pike fishing days were really just beginning but they were very much in earnest. The general run of pike at the pond was in the 3–8lb category with not many of the bigger ones either. However, day after day in the far reed bay what appeared to be a very large fish indeed struck continually in to the shoals of small perch, roach and rudd. The problem was that there was no way whatsoever of getting a bait out there. I found

a boat but when I tried to float it, it sank within yards. I tried a very heavy lead, but it simply sank into the weed and the bait was pulled behind it. In short, I decided that the pike, large as it was, was way beyond my capabilities.

One autumn day an angler who was quite unknown to me arrived at the lake and proceeded to catch some of the bigger roach that were then present. He set up a pike rod with a small bung and hardly any weight, and set the fish at around 2ft – just shallow enough to skirt the weeds. I remember that he greased

No doubt that this pike fell to a float-fished bait.

the line very carefully and simply lobbed the roach into the water.

Little by little, and using clever sidestrain where necessary, he directed the roach further and further away from the bank. Within ten or fifteen minutes that fish had swum well over 100yd and was in actual fact beginning to plug its way around the bay. I was absolutely amazed, but neither was I particularly surprised when after a few minutes of this a great bow wave appeared behind the bubble float and the roach was taken in a cauldron of exploding water. Getting that pike in through 120yd of weedy water was not easy, but finally the fish appeared at the bank. I carried out the duties with the net.

The fish really was a monster. It weighed 11¼lb! Since then I have used the drifting livebait many times to great effect, both on the shallow Norfolk lakes and Broads but also on the wilder waters of Scotland. Simply, there cannot be a more natural way of presenting a bait to pike over big areas of water.

THE SUNKEN FLOAT PATERNOSTER RIG

Having said that my favourite rig is the float paternoster, it is only fair to say that the sunken float does have its uses and indeed many people do feel it is a more sensitive way of presenting a bait. The diagram (*see* Fig. 31) shows the basic way of setting up the rig which must always be under tension or tangles will ensue. There are, however, many different variations on the actual set-up. The sunken float is always a polyball, easily obtainable at any good tackle shop. In short, the advocates of the sunken float rig would say that it tangles less easily and is more sensitive to a taking fish. Also, exact knowledge of the bottom contour is not as necessary as with the 'floating float'! (I must say, however, that I am not in total agreement with the first two points and I personally feel it is important to know as much about the swim and its depths as possible.)

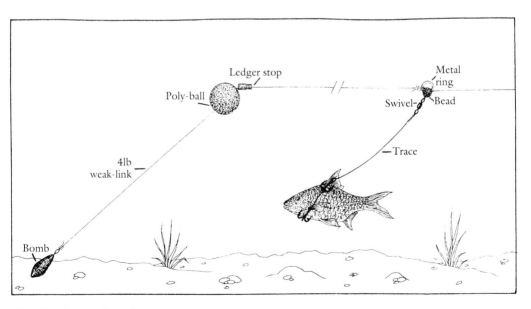

Fig. 31 Sunken float rig.

The sunken float is being used at the moment but the proper float is ready for instant action.

THE FLOAT AND
THE SINK AND DRAW METHOD

Although everybody looking at the sink and draw method will think of its use for pike fishing, a short diversion about a large trout might be quite interesting.

Below a weir on a Scottish river I had seen small trout and salmon parr scatter repeatedly each afternoon as darkness approached. It was quite obvious that a large predator of some sort was on the prowl in that particular area. The centre of the attacks seemed to be in a fairly slow and reasonably deep pool just on the edge of very quick water. I felt that the creature's daytime resting place was deep down under the rocks and that it would then come up to hunt in the higher layers

I only had small deadbaits available to me and I thought these would be best fished with the sink and draw method under a float. My idea was to cast a small dead trout into the flow and then work it back through the deep pool. I decided to wait until I was sure the fish was actually hunting before making my first casts. Sure enough, right on cue, as the sun began to set behind the mountains the first shoal of fish scattered. I cast out into the current and worked the trout back towards me, raising and lowering the rod tip, reeling it back in spurts, imagining the little trout fluttering, rising, falling, twisting and glinting in the last of the light. I did everything to make the fish work as enticingly as possible and on the third cast the slow, heavy pull rewarded my efforts.

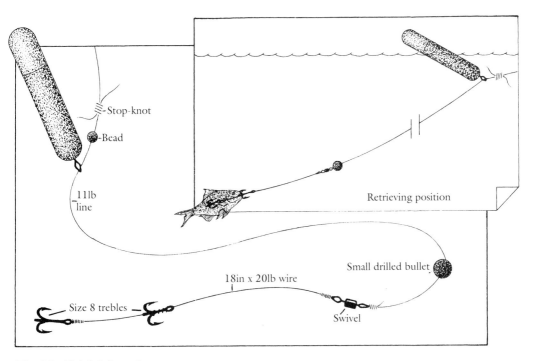

Fig. 32 Sink 'n' draw rig.

The fight, the fish and the whole scene was exhilarating. At just over 10lb, my first large ferox trout was a real reward.

FLOAT FISHING FOR PERCH

The Loafer Float

As far as my experiences go, they tend to suggest that by far the best bait for a big perch is a small livebait of around 2–3in. As to method, the most consistently successful one has been to fish this bait on the move, drifting around a known hot area. To do this properly the bait has to be float fished.

Very probably the best float under which you can present free-roving livebaits is a 3SSG Drennan loafer float. However, I only tend to

weight it with two and not three shots. This is largely to prevent the bait from taking the float under the surface continually – not only frustrating, but continual striking is also harmful to fishing chances and an inch of exposed float tells a lot of tales of action beneath the surface. It is far easier to interpret what a taking fish is doing when there is plenty of float. For example, when the float is lightly shotted it will often tilt one way or the other, or even lie flat as the livebait attempts to escape an attacker. Also, in a wind, the exposed float is that much more visible and movements against the current are more easily detected.

The loafer, being thin, does not put up much resistance in the water as the livebait tows it around. Hence, greater areas of water can be covered – especially if the line is as heavily greased as it should be. Also, on the

A perch surfaces – the loafer
float in evidence.

strike the loafer creates far less resistance than
a traditional pilot or controller float.

It is a good idea to fish the float double
rubber so that a quick change to a heavier or
lighter float can be made. Perch strikes tend
to be rapid and haphazard, and the bait must
be put in the danger area as fast as possible.

Pilot Floats and Floater Controllers

The loafer float is not always suitable for perch
livebaiting, especially in rough weather when
wind and rain can buffet the high-standing
loafer and even blow it flat. The pilot and the
floater controller serve in much the same way
as the loafer but are a little more visible on
dour days. I don't find them as effective under
easier conditions as they offer just that bit of
extra resistance that can make the perch very
finicky. Often this resistance will not matter,
but always err on the side of caution.

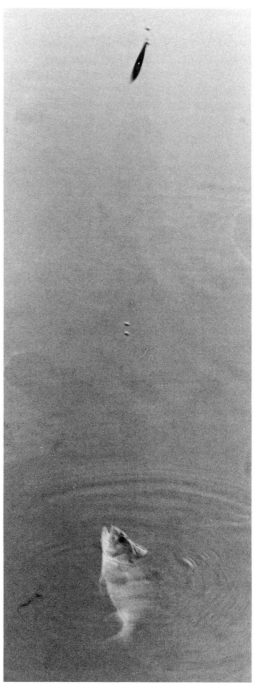

The fish is ready for netting . . .

. . . here it comes.

And it is swung ashore.

This superb pike was taken on a river using the sink and draw method.

8 Float Fishing for Stillwater Species

TENCH

Sadly, over the past twenty years it has become the norm to fish for tench with the lead. Obviously, scaled-down modern carp tactics work very well for big tench and there is no need to ignore them. However, tench have always been caught on the float and they always will be in the future. In part this is an aesthetic thing: there is nothing more fitting than watching the red float against the glow of a June dawn. But there is more to tench float fishing than this. A lot more. Float fishing gives the angler a great variety of attacks and techniques, and opens up many different ways of catching this favourite fish.

The Lift Rig

Traditionally, the float method to use with tench is the lift rig. This is an old method which was described over a century ago as the 'shot ledger', but Fred J. Taylor brought it into the modern world. The float used, in my experience, is either a Drennan driftbeater or a simple section of peacock quill. The important thing is to place the hook around 2in away from the bottom shot. Thereafter, it is one of the most wonderful sights in fishing to see the side bob of a driftbeater float tower out of the water and lie flat on the calm, oily surface. This generally is the time to strike, but there are occasions when it pays to wait a little longer. Why this is so, I do not know, but if the first couple of bites are missed then do experiment. The lift rig generally works best with bigger baits – a piece of buoyant crust is excellent. Also try a size 14 hook for a maggot and brandling cocktail, a size 12 for two grains of sweetcorn or a size 10 or 8 for a full lobworm or big piece of flake.

The lift method can cause problems with bite detection, the main reason for this being that the line from shot to float rises almost vertically in the water. What happens is that when the tench grub around over the bait carpet their bodies and tails brush constantly against the line, moving the float and sometimes even giving false bites. There are a couple of solutions to this problem. One is to move the shot further away from the hook and hope that the tench are feeding hard enough to still give a proper indication. The second way of avoiding these irritations is to lengthen the distance between shot and float so the line cuts through the water at a less acute angle. False bites should then become much less of a problem. If they are still a problem, remember that in reality false bites suggest that your swim is full of fish that are feeding – how can any angler get upset by this?

Laying-On Rig

Another old tench method was the laying-on rig. I say 'was' because it is hardly ever used today – again, probably for no reason. The idea is to set the float a couple of feet overdepth, put all the shot on the bottom 18in away from the hook, and reel tight until the float sits half-cock. A taking tench will then either lie the float flat or slide it straight under.

In practice, and I think it was Len Head who pointed this out, putting all the shot on the bottom can lead to rejected baits. It is probably better to put quite a bit of shot, if not the bulk of it, between the bottom shot and the float. This way less resistance is felt and more tench are hooked safely. This is again an excellent float fishing method with larger baits and should not be neglected.

Floats for Tench

Most of the traditional float rigs were designed for use with large baits, but the whole concept of baits has moved on dramatically in the last few years. Small baits – particles – have become firmly established not only in the carp scene but also in the tench world, and very often the traditional float rigs do not work particularly well with maggots, casters or even single grains of sweetcorn. This is when the tench angler will have to resort to the more modern, more delicate floats and float fishing methods.

There is today a massive selection of very delicate waggler floats on the market, and now the tench angler has a whole range of the most sensitive tools with which to work. My own personal favourites are the crystal wagglers, made virtually invisible by their construction of transparent plastic. I really do believe that this aspect of the crystals is important. I have no doubt that tench in clear water can see the typical float and, when well educated, know how to avoid the entire area. I am not saying the crystal is invisible, but it does seem to fool tench a great deal longer.

The diagram (*see* Fig. 33) explains the traditional placing of the bulk shot, but I think it really is a matter for your own preference. Matchmen tend to place the bulk shot around the float as locking shot. This means that the float tends to precede the bait in flight and a slight 'feathering' is required to prevent tangles. The main reason for doing this is that the bait drops slowly through the water and can be intercepted by fish on the drop. Obviously, when tench fishing this rarely happens (although it does happen sometimes), so for general use it is probably easier to place the bulk shot lower down the line as in the diagram.

The straight crystal waggler is obviously not suitable all the time. If bites are very

Fig. 33 A waggler set-up for big fish.

A tench and float in the net.

finicky then it might pay to change over to the slightly more sensitive insert crystal waggler. The tip of this is noticeably finer than that of the ordinary waggler and therefore less resistance is set up. In practice, however, I find that this refinement is seldom necessary when tench fishing.

More importantly, there are times when a change of float pattern is required. This is generally when there is a fair amount of wind on the water which in turn produces an undertow. The traditional waggler can be pulled out of position by this undertow, and a windbeater is probably the best float to use under these circumstances. Shotted as the diagram suggests (*see* Fig. 2) this rig really does perform as its name promises so that it is possible to fish tightly under the most dire of conditions.

I did say that sometimes a drifting float can be an advantage. Just occasionally I have known tench to prefer to take a moving bait rather than a stationary one. Once again, I have no idea why this should be but it is worth trying if bites are slow and the wind is high. An onion-type float is ideal for this method. It needs to be set 18–20in deeper than the swim with a small shot resting on the bottom some 6in from the hook. You actually allow the line to float and catch the wind to help tow the float through the swim. Obviously, the bottom needs to be fairly clear of weed and in practice the bottom shot does tend to get caught up. The float tends to sink and draw under the surface a fair bit, but generally this movement is very slow and hesitant. A tench bite is much more positive as the fish intercepts the bait and moves off with it –

Big tench adore warm, weedy water.

hopefully confidently. I emphasize that this is not a method on which I have caught a lot of tench, but I have known it work on occasion – and, of course, it is impossible to present the moving bait with a ledger!

When fishing the crystal waggler under normal conditions I very often (if not usually) suspend the bait about ½in off the bottom. Exact depth plumbing is vital for this because float setting is crucial. The reasons for lifting the bait minutely off the bottom are twofold. First, tench often seem to like a bait so positioned. Again, I do not know why this is so, but perhaps in the turmoil down there with the silt being stirred from the paddle-like pectorals, a bait so presented is a little bit more visible. Second, when an off-bottom bait is taken, the float cannot help but register the bite . . . something that does not always happen when the bait is on the bottom. It is simply amazing how easily a tench can accept and then eject a bait with hardly any indication on the float.

There are times when tench will take baits in mid-water. I have seen this happen quite frequently, especially at the start of the season when the water is warm and the tench do seem to be particularly hungry. Naturally heavy baiting with small particles is virtually essential for this to happen. Maggots, casters and hemp in significant quantities can all raise tench up from the bottom and make them jostle for the offerings in mid-water, or even a few inches beneath the float. In these circumstances freelining a bait is possible if the water is very clear, visibility is good and the tench are in close. In practice, a float is more often necessary. I find that any very small float will do for this job and at times I have even been quite happy with a simple matchstick. However, for those wanting a little more sophistication there are several dibbler-type floats now on the market which serve the purpose just as well. If you have the tench feeding in this way at range,

then obviously a larger float carrying some shot will be necessary. Again, the crystal waggler is all that you are likely to need, with all the shot pushed up around the float so that the bait can fall freely through the water. It is an amazing method and heart-stoppingly exciting to see big tench rolling just under the surface and walloping into the feed. It is also surprising but true that large bream will often join in the game.

It is very usual that tench seek out the weediest part of the water, especially when the sun is high and their patrolling has come to an end. It is often possible to see individual fish moving through slight gaps in the weed, and they will often stop to pick up a bait – especially if it is a sizeable or attractive one. What I like to do is use either a piece of peacock or a very small waggler. I then plumb the depth and set the float exactly to that level. A large bait such as a piece of flake or lobworm will then at least half-cock the float and sometimes cock it completely. No weights are necessary, and the rig is simply lobbed out into the hole and rod put on rest . . . the wait then begins. Bites are usually ultra-confident and the float just zips under. It is necessary to be alert and strike at once or the fish might well get a couple of yards away from you under yet more weed. The secret is to hit, hold and hustle the fish to the top. Fairly strong tackle is obviously necessary, but you can often get away with this method in places where the tench rarely expect to be ambushed.

CARP

It is not the place of this book to question modern-day attitudes and ethics, simply to comment on the best ways of using floats in special situations. I will, however, say that it is sad that the modern-day carp scene seems to be so dominated by leads and ledger techniques, for some of the best carp that I have ever caught have been taken on the float in situations where no other technique would have worked properly.

Laying-On Technique

Perhaps the most conventional way of float fishing for carp is to lay on. This is the simplest possible method, but vital points to consider are that the line from rod tip to float must be kept as tight as conditions allow and also that the rod is always held in the hands. It is amazing how quickly a carp can pick up and eject a bait, and very frequently a rapid strike must be made. I lay on in many situations, especially close to the bank where the entry of a lead would be obtrusive in the extreme. The laying-on technique is also very useful when fishing a bait close to a snag. With standard rigs the bait can be picked up and carp can very often make sanctuary before a strike is made. When laying-on, however, as soon as the float dips, the carp is hooked and can be hustled away from danger. Laying-on is also very useful with particle baits that can often be swallowed or ejected on conventional methods before there is any real indication. Also, most waters are used to modern lead techniques and frequently something a little bit different can pay dividends . . . enter the float.

In winter 1987 I fished a very hard, small pit for carp. My target was an uncaught 20lb fish, but I would have been pleased with any of the other carp in there. At first I fished with methods typical of the summer – boilies, hairs, bolt rigs and the like – and failed utterly. Only late one afternoon did I see some carp activity, tucked tight in to some low, sweeping alders. I crept round to them; the water was opaque, the light was dim and I could just make out the slow-moving bodies of some five or six fish – mostly commons

with perhaps two mirrors amongst them. The next afternoon I was back, but with perhaps the most unusual carp bait used that year on the water – a bucket of bread, mashed and flavoured with maple.

For two hours, I sat in the alders baiting an area a rod length before me. The roach went crazy, splashing, rolling and gorging on the stuff. This was my intention: to stimulate a feeding frenzy that would transmit to the carp. After an hour a carp did appear on the scene and then two more. The roach grew scarce, pushed from the area by the bigger fish. A common carp head and shouldered, and bubbles appeared in patches of fizz. The time had come. My bait was flavoured flake on a size 6 hook, 2in beneath the swan shot and above that an ordinary quill float. The rod was held in my hands and the float was cocked on a tight line. Five minutes and then ten minutes passed, my left hand constantly feeding in dribbles of bread. Then, as quick as the blink of an eye, the float was flat, the rod hooped and the water an angry foam. It was not the 20lb fish but a good one just the same.

As the week progressed, several more carp were taken from the same swim on the same bait using the same technique whilst very close at hand; the traditional boilie set-up went untouched.

Stalking Carp

I cannot remember when I was last carp fishing without a rod made up for stalking. Generally I use the windbeater float as this is very stable in larger, open, windy waters. For this reason, notice the small backstop in the diagram (*see* Fig. 3): this sinks the line and makes the whole rig even less prone to drifting. The windbeater is a very delicate and precise float, and it can be shotted so that even the quickest bite is registered.

A carp like this can eject a bait in seconds.

An opportunist fish this one, picked up from the shallows.

The advantage of the windbeater lies in its precision. A particular 22lb fish sticks in my memory. I found him grazing the flats early one July morning, meandering very slowly, and feeding heavily as he went. Small silt clouds ballooned after him and patches of bubbles blew up close by. I knew that if a lead had dropped close to this fish he would have bolted. A lead cast ahead of him could have been yards off course, its position lost to my eye in the silt, and impossible to reposition without disturbing the fish. The float though landed 3yd ahead of the fish, silently enough to have been a twig from the nearby oak tree. I waited until the fish approached and simply manoeuvred the float to within a foot of the fish's head. In twenty seconds the carp was over the bait, under the float and the tip of red was gone – neat, effective simplicity and the only carp of the session.

For the carp stalker, the traditional float can be married to the modern shock rig with devastating results. A near-30lb fish in summer 1987 was a particular victim of the method. I had spotted the carp in a quiet corner of a pool, almost totally surrounded by branches and big fallen trees. There was no bankside swim from which I could approach the area so I was forced to fish from the tree that I had climbed earlier in order to spot the fish. Fishing presented all manner of problems. The water was quite deep – around 7ft – and the wind was piling up into the swim, blowing debris and masking the water clarity. The swim was also a nightmare of snags and the carp, if it was going to take the bait, would have to be hooked and held on the spot. I had one advantage: a small table-top of clean-swept sand set amidst the general backdrop of silt and mud had to be the carp's main feeding

The carp stalker!

area. A bait placed there would have to be seen – at least eventually. I had to hold the rod – obviously rests were out as I was up a tree, and the float was the indicator. Equally though, I needed the fish to hook itself, as a strike in those trees would be difficult or impossible. I placed the bomb 5in from the hook and the whole rig was swung underarm on to the sand. The use of the float in this way also allowed me to know that the bait was positioned with absolute accuracy.

The big carp was still in the area and, although spotting was a hit-and-miss affair, every few minutes a gleam, a heavy flat patch on the surface, or an area of bubbles betrayed its presence. An hour on, the bubbles became a constant stream over and around my sand bar. Then there was a gleam beneath the float, I tensed and, just as I had hoped, the float dived, the rod bucked and I was in, playing

the fish directly from the elevated position in the pine tree. From above, I kept a tight rein on the carp and hammered it from the encompassing snags. Within minutes it was wallowing in the net and a pretty little plan had, for once succeeded.

Very often, especially towards midmorning when the main feeding spell is over and the heat is growing, carp come off the bottom and patrol around in mid-water or near the surface. They are no longer really hungry but they can still be tempted into taking the occasional morsel of food, providing it is easily within their range of vision. Therefore, a bait placed several feet beneath the fish is almost certainly going to be ignored, whereas a slowly sinking bait could well be taken. A worm, a piece of breadflake or even a couple of grains of sweetcorn are ideal for this approach and at fairly short range any of these can be presented under a self-cocking float. At longer ranges a bubble float is ideal. It can be filled with water to give an exceptional casting range and it will not scare the fish – indeed, carp will often mouth at it out of curiosity! This is a method that really does work and can extend the morning fishing session by quite some time. Again, the float is absolutely essential for success.

A float can be the most primitive of things, providing it does its job. In the summer of 1991 I had the opportunity to fish a 2-acre lake that was extremely shallow at that particular time as there had been little rain and much water abstraction in the area. As a result, the carp kept under an extensive lily bed throughout the daylight hours, and I could see the pads rising and falling as their bodies squirmed beneath them in the bottom silt. Traditional methods were completely out: it is simply not possible to cast a ledger rig into the middle of dense lilies. What I could see was a possibility, however, was to swing a bait into a small opening on the edge of the pads where bodies could frequently be seen gliding past. I simply attached a small twig on to the line with a float rubber and set it around 15in from the hook. A piece of luncheon meat was swung 5yd out into the opening and the twig lay poised on the edge of the lily pad. Half an hour passed, the carp entered the clearing and the twig flicked off the pad into the water. An instant strike and sidestrain pulled the fish from the lily bed, and within a minute what was a good carp for the water was netted.

Floats and lily pads seem to go together. Floating baits themselves are often rejected and a bottom-fished bait generally sinks into the mass of roots and is ignored. However, a bait fished at mid-water under a float is a different proposition and is very frequently taken, even though the set-up looks ridiculous superficially. It is amazing how often even a boilie dangling 2ft under a float will be picked up in the heat of a summer's afternoon. Even in open water this will often work, and for no reason at all a passing carp will simply engulf a mid-water bait.

The attentive carp angler knows that carp really do scrape reed stems for the life that clings there, and often they will feed this way later on in the afternoon, well before sunset. A small, natural bait often works well at these times and I have caught carp on maggots, redworms and brandlings in particular. The best method is to fish them hard against the reed stems some way off the bottom – a float makes this type of presentation ideal. A quill cannot be bettered for the job, but in my experience it should be fixed on the line by both top and bottom rubbers. If it is attached to the line by a bottom rubber only, there is the ever-present risk of it catching or snagging between the stems when a fish runs. When fastened top and bottom, however, the float hugs the line and follows it through the reeds in a more streamlined and less dangerous fashion.

There is no doubt in my mind that often carp will be put on guard by the presence of line in the water close to a bait. In summer 1989, for instance, carp after carp approached my fishing area only to bolt away when they saw or felt the line from the rod tip to the lead and the bait. I did find a way round this without using the float: leaving my rod on the bank with the bail arm of the reel open, I carried the worm and the lead over to an island, wading up to about waist-deep through silt and the warm water. At the island, I laid the worm 5yd off the far side, then tucked the line in close to the overgrown banking for 20yd and finally trod down the line from island to rod into the bottom weed as best I could. I hoped that hardly any line would be visible to passing fish, and I dried off in the sun and sat back. I had a durable bait in a good area with the line hidden down for most of its length.

A small carp taken on float-fished corn.

I had to wait some time, but at last the passing carp were not frightened and eventually one took the bait. The lesson was an obvious one: tight lines in mid-water spell danger to anything like a wary fish. Again this is where a float can come in. If the line is greased to the float so that it lies on the surface, the carp can approach the bait without realizing there is any danger at all. Of course, when a wary fish gets so close it might well see the line coming vertically down from the float, but at least it has not been spooked up to that point and a take is still possible.

The great beauty about float fishing for carp is that there are no real rules and the angler can be totally adaptable to the water, the fish, the weather and the whole situation as he meets it. There is immense satisfaction in thinking about a particularly difficult carp fishing scenario and plotting its solution – especially when the float is central to the success of the whole escapade.

CRUCIAN CARP

I rather feel that crucian carp will become one of the cult species as the end of the century advances. Several waters now hold crucians far in excess of the present record, and more and more specialist anglers are coming to realize just how worthy these amazing fish are. They are not only beautiful and cunning, but now are also large.

I should stress the word 'cunning'. Arguably, there is no more difficult fish to catch than the crucian carp. In part this is due to a wariness of all baits, but it also stems from the intricacies of the crucian's feeding habits. Many years ago I kept a pet crucian in a tank by the side of my bed and would spend many happy hours watching it fed in a natural, happy-go-lucky sort of way. What was immediately obvious was the fact that this crucian would suck and blow at a piece of food for often half a dozen times before finally swallowing it. I cannot believe that the fish was checking for tackle or anything like that, but was perhaps softening up the bait before taking it down to its throat teeth. Whatever the reason, this pattern was almost an invariable one. Possibly, in the wild the competition of other shoal members cuts down the number of times a bait is rejected before being finally swallowed, but I'm sure that in principle the same habit that I witnessed also exists there. In fact, in one particular clear and shallow lake I have actually seen wild crucian adopt this same habit.

A beautiful wildie is returned.

Now, considering all this, it becomes quite obvious that fishing methods have to be refined considerably in order to cope. In my view, ledgering is virtually a nonsense and it is interesting that whilst carp anglers may catch a lot of bream, tench or even roach by accident on their boilies and hair rigs, we rarely hear of a huge crucian being landed in this way. As far as I'm concerned, no ledger rig is nearly flexible enough to cope with a crucian carp.

So, we have to look at floats – which is, after all, really the right way a crucian should be caught! There are fairly obvious guide-lines when choosing the crucian float. You will almost certainly be fishing in a stillwater, so it is highly likely that you will be looking for a waggler-type set-up. Also, bearing in mind the crucian's feeding habits, it is wise to have the slimmest float possible and one with perhaps a long antenna which would be capable of signalling the most gentle bites in an obvious fashion. Generally, I find that crucian swims are very close to the bank simply because the species seems to love the shelter of overhanging trees. Weed will do, but nothing seems to please crucians more than a protective canopy of wood and leaf! It is my belief that in many cases crucians abhor the sunlight, and in actual fact will move around a swim to get away from the sun as it moves in the sky. This tendency to hug the bank means that most crucians in my experience can be caught one or two lengths out – this again means that a light and delicate float can be used as long casting is generally unnecessary. Several floats would fit the bill – stillwater blues, an insert crystal perhaps, a canal crystal, a dart or one of the grey range with the very long stems.

The caution of crucians tends to fade to some degree with the onset of darkness. Very frequently a water that has been virtually fed all day will come alive at around 10 p.m. on a July

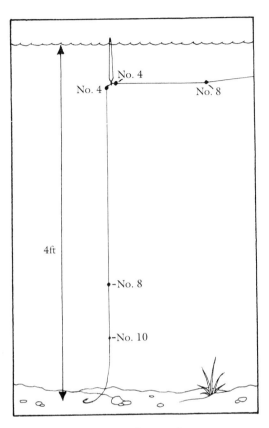

Fig. 34 The tapered balsa waggler.

or August night. Float fishing is still almost mandatory and little can beat a giant crystal. Bites that were very finicky during the day frequently become far bolder in the darkness and there is little mistake when a fish has taken the bait.

During the daytime, it can be a problem to decide when to strike a crucian bite. Laying-on is probably as sound a method as there is, and I tend to wait until the float has lifted by ½in and seems to be continuing. The other method, if the wind and surface tow is very slight, is to fish the bait fractionally above bottom. And I mean fractionally – ½in is about right. Bites then tend to be signalled by a slow dip as the float trundles away.

BREAM

There is no doubt about it: the crystal floats have been a great step forward for all of us. They emerged from that very fruitful mind of Peter Drennan. The story is told that he was fishing a clear pit in the margins for tench with John Everard. They were on a high bank and the weather was bright and sunny. The tench were very clever, old fish and both anglers, good as they were, were struggling for success. The fish were there though, and could be seen moving around from the left in water about 5–6ft deep. There was a certain amount of tow on the water and both men were using large peacocks around 4yd out over the second shelf. They had scattered a few bits of breadflake around to stop the tench but not overfeed them. The floats were about 3–4yd apart and the tench could be seen clearly going down in the general area. Both John and Peter were tense, especially as there were odd indications on the float indicating line bites.

Finally, all activity ceased and John climbed the bank and looked into the swim: 'They've bloody gone!' Both men were obviously disappointed and wondered why.

The wind had dropped right off, and as it was noon the water was very bright. They looked hard and then saw that all the pieces of flake had gone, but for two. The two hookbaits were sitting there, proudly white against the bottom. Oh, and one free offering was right next to one of the hookbaits. It was obvious that the tench would not go under the floats. The anglers were using black-bottomed quills and it had to be that they were the problem and not the hooks themselves at all.

In water this clear, a crystal float makes sense.

Obviously, the pair could have gone on to the lead or fished a float crazily overdepth to get the bait well away. Neither idea appealed, and so Drennan began to develop the clear-bodied float. Thus the crystal was born.

Now, that is some introduction to this type of float but the model certainly deserves it. I use crystals a great deal in my tench fishing, but they are equally as good for bream. My local lake is a case in point. It tends to be extremely clear with a wide marginal shelf about 2ft gradually sloping down into deeper water of some 5–6ft. The bream average 5–7lb but there are certainly many doubles and probably one or two knocking 13lb or 14lb. They have been around for a long time and they know virtually all the tricks in the game.

The general method is to fish the drop-off between the shelf and the deep water in around 3–4ft of this very clear water. There is absolutely no doubt in my mind that traditional dark-bodied floats scare those fish. You can actually see them come into the swim and make a wide detour so as to avoid the float. They see it, it spells danger to them and they clear off. It's as simple as that.

With the crystal, however, things are much different. The incoming bream seem oblivious to the float and are quite happy to feed underneath it where they will give, on occasion, resounding bites.

As the day develops the bream tend to move quite a way further out into much deeper water. During this period I frequently change over to the loaded crystal with the bulk weight screwed into the bottom. I do this for the much greater casting distance this model gives me. It flies absolutely straight and accurate with no casting effort whatsoever. The only problem with it is that it dives more deeply through the water upon entry than the traditional floats do. The same aerodynamics that allow it to fly so easily through the air also allow it to penetrate the surface of the water

with greater effect. For this reason, the loaded crystal is of little use on the shelf itself. It will actually dive on to the bream and obviously spook the fish very quickly.

Very often a northerly wind springs up on this particular lake as the day develops. It is close to the coast and on hot days cooler air seems to funnel in. Drag then becomes a problem and I will probably move up from a 2g crystal waggler to a 3g crystal waggler. The latter is some 2in longer than the former and the length itself seems to keep the float more stable. If the wind gets up even more, then I will probably move on to a bodied crystal which has quite a few of the properties of a driftbeater without the top sight bob. If a real wind develops then I will have to move on to the driftbeater to stand any chance of keeping the bait stable. It is not something I like to do, but the bream themselves seem to be less cautious when there is a real chop on the water. A good wind also begins to cloud the lake to some degree and makes the driftbeater that much less obvious.

Of course, I often use swimfeeders for the bream and they can be very effective indeed. However, on the shallow shelf the splash of the feeders does frequently unsettle both bream and trench. Also, I like to use a float as I get a perfect picture of the area of lake I am fishing, and whilst the float is in the water I can feed very carefully with a steady rain of maggots, corn or wheat, and I know exactly where to aim for. It must also be said that the bream have developed some type of wariness of the ledger method – bites are not always positive and I have the feeling that they have worked the method out. It could be that because swimfeeders tend to demand more line in the water the bream feel it on their backs and this alarms them. I don't know, but I am aware that the float often brings more and better bites. Indeed, when the water is relatively calm it is possible to use an insert

A scale-perfect bream.

crystal which really magnifies the bites no end, until they become almost unmissable.

This is quite an important point: we all know the real problems of line bites and missed bites when bream ledgering is used. I find that on the float a bite nearly always means a fish on the bank. The float generally seems to give me a great deal of time and I find that I can really make my mind up when to strike. I'm not saying that this is not the case when ledgering, but somehow a float really screams out at you. The strike is quite important and I like a slow, steady, powerful sweep backwards, keeping the rod as low to the water as possible. I still think it is important to pull the line through the water rather than up in the water – if you see what I mean! Undoubtedly, more power goes into the actual strike that way rather than simply displacing water.

Of course, at night it is quite simple to substitute the crystal for a night float with a Beta-light in the top. I find a 300 Microlambert isotope quite enough for most of my fishing, even at quite long range. Indeed, these are so bright that it is often possible to see them from the other bank! I generally like to use quite heavy mainline with one of these floats as they are quite valuable and a big carp or sizeable tench can come along at any time after dark. Losing a fish is bad enough without seeing an expensive float disappear off down the lake as well! The use of a fairly heavy mainline demands quite a large float to balance it, but this rarely matters after dark and, as usual, it is better to be somewhat over-gunned than undergunned.

On this same lake and on many others, the bream will come in very close at night if there is any reasonable depth of water in the margins. The dam wall sees a lot of bream activity in the first two or three hours of darkness, and it is possible to get away with quite a light night float virtually under the rod tip. This is one of the most exciting ways of fishing. The float glows, bobs, sways around and generally behaves like some drunken ghost when the bream come into the swim and disturb the water around it. Then the float goes – you can even see it burning dimly as it plummets towards the bottom! It is exciting fishing – especially when a 12lb bream could be the culprit.

RUDD

The whole art of fishing for rudd has changed dramatically since the 1950s. Once upon a time, back in the days of Crabtree, most people thought of rudd as surface feeders and fished for them accordingly. However, with the advent of modern specimen hunting in the 1960s, rudd were treated like any other species. The method for catching them became the traditional long-range ledgering technique. Most big fish appeared to be caught at night, often on the ridges of gravel bars and on baits that could just as easily have been picked up by tench or bream. More large two-pounders and three-pounders have been landed over the last twenty years than ever before – and that is even taking into account the relative decline in numbers of these beautiful fish. However, the long-range ledgering technique rates low on the 'fun' side. It is frequently hard, boring work, and there are more interesting and much more selective approaches.

It is very interesting to watch a shoal of rudd in the sunlight. The fish tend either to hang up under weed or fallen trees, or to move quite briskly around the water. Typically, a shoal of good fish will number between five and thirty and will be quite unmistakable on a bright day in clear water. They will create a whole moving spectrum of flashing reds and golds that is marvellous to behold! Whilst they are on the move in this way they will take a bait present-ed in the upper or middle layers of the water and will be totally oblivious to food on the bed. A typical day with this type of movement will probably see a fairly brisk wind which, I believe, cools the water for them to some extent and perhaps even blows terrestrial insects on to the surface – a food source that obviously attracts them.

These fish, therefore, are obviously catch-able – especially on the float. Obviously, too, you need the bulk of the shot as trapping shot and must allow the bait to fall as naturally and as unhampered as possible. A self-cocking float is not a bad idea in itself.

Whatever float you decide to use, the cast-ing weight is an absolutely vital consideration. It is essential to cast way beyond the moving shoal, and to pull the float and bait back into its path. I cannot overemphasize how cau-tious a shoal of rudd will be, and it will cer-tainly never tolerate a float falling on top of it. You are unlikely to take more than one to three fish before the shoal moves away, and even this number depends on the shoal size and how far away from it you are fishing. Obviously, it makes sense to travel as light as possible so that you can keep in touch with the travelling group of fish. Polaroid glasses and binoculars are absolutely essential aids for this type of fishing.

In the summer of 1992 I heard that rudd were back on one of Norfolk's largest broads in some numbers and some size. The water is one of several hundred acres and obviously the ledgering approach was just not feasible. Fishing blind on such a massive stillwater would have been totally foolish. I mentioned

A wonderful rudd.

Crabtree earlier: his technique on such a water was to place floating bread in the marginal reeds which was tethered by string to a stone. Quite how he managed this in the 1940s and 1950s, I am not sure; I am convinced there were just as many waterfowl in Broadland then as now, and my initial researches into the technique proved that tethered bread lasted something in the region of two to three minutes! It was certainly devoured long before a rudd shoal could appear. However, the technique did get me afloat and obviously boat fishing was absolutely essential on such a water.

The only successful technique was to get out there in the middle of the broad and watch the rudd through binoculars. Dawn was a reasonable period, but there were better times still. For example, a very hot, still,

clear day could produce rudd sightings in the early to mid-afternoon. But best of all were the hot, still dusks when the sun seemed to take an eternity to sink and the air was absolutely alive with midges. There were occasions when the whole vast area of the broad would seem like a shimmering cauldron freckled with the rings of rising fish. This was a problem in itself: I needed to take great care to identify the rudd and not confuse them with the bream. A major guide to this seems to be that rudd roll in a much more splashy way and frequently come half-clear of the water. By contrast, the typical bream roll is a much smoother, more porpoise-like affair. Seen through binoculars the difference shows up even more starkly.

You really need a typical, modern float rod for this type of fishing. You will also need 4lb

Alan Rawden with just a couple of his immense rudd.

double-strength line straight through to the hook, a good heavy float and a size 12 hook which will be baited with flake or perhaps three or four maggots. With this sort of gear you can achieve fabulous casting distances and you've still got the muscle to extract a good sized fish from even fairly weedy water. Binoculars are again a vital aid to watching the float as the light decreases. In fact, you can pursue the rudd right into the semi-darkness as their feeding becomes more and more frantic, until sometimes you only know you have a bite because the rod tip pulls around the side of the boat! This is very beautiful and very exciting fishing with some very big fish coming out too. I honestly feel that these Broadland rudd could *only* have been caught on the float and that the standard specimen method really would have been totally futile in the pursuit of these wonderful fish.

EELS

Everybody knows that big eels feed at night on the bottom on chunks of fish or bunches of worms. Everybody also knows that eels are sinister, grubbing, sinuous creatures of the underwater world. But everybody is wrong, or at least half-wrong! The old concept of the lurking eel is not always correct, and recent observations and research have proved that a great many eels are in actual fact browsers, living on *daphnia* and small insects. These eels tend to develop smaller, narrower heads that are better adapted to sipping small creatures from weeds or from under stones.

I myself watched such an eel for over two months during 1990. Its behaviour, clearly seen in an almost transparent lake, was absolutely fascinating. I guessed the fish (for I never caught it) weighed about 3lb and during all that time it inhabited one small area of the lake about the size of an average dining room. Day after day during bright sunlight that eel would be visible, but it had a definite life plan. It would sulk for around an hour under the shade of thick weed, but then it would come out and feed voraciously for forty-five to sixty minutes. *Daphnia* were one of its favourite targets but passing waterboatmen, beetles and freshwater shrimps were equally acceptable. The fish worked constantly, wriggling and writhing, snapping and supping – in fact, in these feeding frenzies it was every bit as active as any 'normal' fish. Frequently I threw in a large piece of food – a large lobworm, or a dead minnow, for example – and this would be totally ignored. However, as soon as I threw in half a dozen maggots they would be wolfed down.

Now, I never bothered to even try and catch this eel – it even became something of a pet and I looked after it most days when I visited the lake in search of one of the huge carp there. However, had the eel been 6lb, say, then my approach might have been a little bit different! What I have no doubt about is that that fish would easily have been caught on a normal float fished with the maggot technique. I would have used a waggler with most of the weight as trap shot and very little else down the line, so that the bait would have sunk under its own weight and settled on top of the weed rather than burrowing into it.

Obviously, specialist eel hunters do catch a number of big eels but I do wonder how many of the narrow-headed type they miss. In fact, shortly before his tragic death, I was talking to John Sidley about this very subject. I remember him being wildly excited at the concept of fishing for eels with small baits and even with floats in the method I have described. He felt that small-headed eels grew to just the same size as large-headed eels, if not bigger, and he felt that a whole new chapter in eel fishing was opening up for him. How sad that this exciting departure should

The type of water where a big eel will feed on small insects.

have been taken away from him at a cruelly young age. What John would have wanted me to have written in this book – and indeed what he stressed to me himself – was that the technique demands a quick strike. If the strike were delayed for any length of time then the hook would be into the eel's throat or stomach; a dead eel is something none of us wants.

Of course, the other type of eel (commonly thought of as the broad-headed species) are fish-eaters. These are the eels that generally fall to the traditional specialist approach of ledgering large baits close to snags at night. However, even these can be far more active hunters than most people realize. I remember being afloat on the Broads one hot August day searching for tench swims. What I saw that afternoon has stayed with me ever since. In some areas the bays were full of large eels swimming a few inches beneath the surface, actively hunting that year's stock of fingerling bream and roach. For all the world, they were acting like shoals of perch on the prowl. That, I hasten to add, is not an isolated incident and over the years I have seen many more eels behave in such a way.

Also vivid is the memory of a large eel in a north Norfolk pond that stationed itself at the mouth of an outlet pipe. This area, under an alder tree, seemed to attract the fingerling

carp, and the big eel would hover like a floating stick and then arrow out into any congregation of small fish. It did not always make a kill, but several times I saw it retreat with just a tail visible from its mouth.

It would seem after all these sightings that there are other approaches to big eels than the simple, ledgered deadbaits in the depths of the night. How about a suspended livebait or deadbait under a small float, perch fashion? Of course, resistance would be the major problem that any enterprising eel angler would face. I suspect that a very quick strike would be essential before the eel spat out the bait. Perhaps a 2in fish with a hook in the mouth and one half-way down the back would be the answer, so that an instant strike could be made. In this way, at least one hook would be bound to catch somewhere in the eel's mouth. I am not sure if the eel has a preferred target area, but two hooks on a small bait should cover most of the body.

I appreciate that both of these methods are very experimental. However, considering the number of very large eels that are present in British waters, a pitiful score of them is caught every decade. Perhaps it is time for the stereotyped eel angler to widen his horizons just that little bit and actually buy in a stock of floats!

9 Float Fishing for River Species

CHUB

I have already mentioned in a previous chapter that chub can often be caught on the float in far greater numbers than on the lead.

Indeed, it is my frequent experience that chub that have been hard fished for will often be very wary of a static bait. This is the standard approach and the chub know it. The rolling ledger can pick up some fish but it

Perfect stick float water.

does have many presentation problems. It is difficult, for example, to roll a ledger on an exactly straight course, and it is not long in the average river before the ledger begins to pick up a great deal of debris. Freelining is also a good way to take chub under many conditions, but bite indication can be a problem: not all chub grab the bait with gusto and really tear off as they should do!

This leaves the float, and what a joy it is to catch chub from close in on the stick float. From the Wensum to the Wye, with many in between, I have had some of my most pleasurable chub fishing close in to my own bank, working a stick float carefully through eddies, along creases and close to snags. There is no doubt that chub respond eagerly to steady feeding with maggots, casters, hemp and even tares. Soon a shoal will begin to forage actively for food, leave the snags and rise up in the water. This is where the stick float really wins. It is delicate and precise, and when held back the bait rises enticingly, straight into the mouth of a fish dashing past.

So many chub swims are absolutely made for the stick-float approach. A fallen tree or bush on your own bank can be attacked so well by allowing the stick float to inch past it. You can really cover the water and put your bait in front of every fish in the shoal. Consider the activity and excitement this approach generates down in the swim . . . fish everywhere chasing the falling maggots and slowly sinking casters, chub rooting on the bottom, flashing in mid-water and even occasionally bulging at the surface. A fish has very little time to inspect a bait or one of its shoal partners will take it first. So, providing the bait is reasonably well presented (and what does this better than a stick float), it is very likely to be taken without any hesitation.

Contrast this situation with the normal specialist approach: two, four or six large chunks of luncheon meat sit on the bottom, one firmly attached to a size 6 hook and a ledger weight a few inches away. The odd chub leaves the safety of the snag and perhaps mouths a free offering. It is taken. A few minutes later another fish comes out and gingerly takes a second piece. All is quiet for ten or fifteen minutes when the third loose offering is taken. The angler reels in to check his bait and all the chub see that happen.

The angler then casts again and the piece of meat on the lead falls to the bottom in a totally unnatural fashion. All the chub, especially the largest ones, mark this well. Two or three new pieces of luncheon meat are thrown in as loose offerings. They fall to the bottom differently and a smaller chub sidles out to take one. Twenty minutes go by and the angler reels in his bait, concludes that there are no chub in the swim or that they are not feeding and goes down to try the next swim.

I know that not all fishing is described as simply as this, but there is more than an element of truth in the scenario that I have painted so that hopefully some of the traditional ledger men will think again.

I once watched a quite superb exhibition of float fishing on the River Kennet. The river was quite narrow, fairly clear and fairly quick, and the angler was fishing a snag on the bank opposite. This was a tree whose branches hung within 3ft of the water surface and whose roots extended well out. Quite a few chub lived under those roots, reputedly one or two large ones.

The angler's approach was to settle himself down opposite the roots and feed heavily with hemp and casters quite a way upriver so they drifted past the chubs' home. He fed for some ten to fifteen minutes and then set up using a medium-sized waggler. He cast this 4–5yd upstream of the snags so that the bait had reached the bottom by the time it was opposite the roots. There was no need to mend line, and all he had to do was keep in touch with

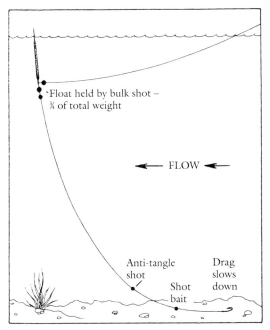

Float held by bulk shot –
¾ of total weight

◄— FLOW ◄—

Anti-tangle
shot

Drag
slows
down

Shot
bait

Fig. 35 A waggler rig explained.

the float. For cast after cast, by the time the float had reached the snags and moved a foot or two it would simply disappear. All in all, by using the waggler this chap had eight chub out before lunchtime.

All this took place while I found the most perfect chub swim imaginable. I tackled it traditionally on the lead and my reward was a two-pounder, landed just before dusk fell! There is no doubt in my mind that in those cold, clear and difficult conditions the chub wanted small baits moving naturally rather than one large bait tethered unnaturally. The waggler approach was perfect for that particular swim, and the angler's control of float and bait was remarkable.

During the summer of 1986 I spent quite a few days on the River Lugg. This is a beautiful chub stream, not very wide but full of variety. There are deeps, pools, bends and long straights, all carpeted in gravel and blossoming with weed. It was possible to pick chub up

virtually everywhere using a wide variety of methods. One of the most successful was to catch the fish at range using large pieces of breadflake.

On this day I began by taking them off the top on floating crust, but soon they began to wise up to this and started to prefer the sunken bread. I tried freelining the flake but it tended to sink and get caught up in the weed. I also noticed that I was missing a few bites. The answer was to use a loafer float, which I set to mid-range carrying around 2½ swan shot. A swan each side of the float acted as trapping shot, with just a couple of BBs half-way between the float and hook. The hook was a size 8 and the flake was quite a large piece. The runs were around 5ft deep and I set the float at between 3–4ft.

I simply paid out line with the current and found the loafer a very accommodating float to work down the swim. Line mending was very rarely necessary and I could keep perfect control for anything up to 40yd or so. The loafer also allowed me to steer my tackle around the worst of the weedbeds and even skirt down the side of the long beds of ranunculus.

There is no doubt that the chub adore this method. Providing I had put in quite a few free offerings beforehand, a bite was guaranteed the first swim down. And what bites they were! The float would disappear, and sometimes I could even see it cutting across the river below the surface. The only thing was that I had to strike very firmly because frequently the take would be at distance and the loafer itself set up quite a bit of resistance in the water. In short, the loafer seems the perfect float for distance fishing on quick, boisterous rivers when the chub are very active and looking for large lumps of food.

Sadly, however, this is not always the case and frequently chub will only want smaller food items. These do not need to be tiny but they should be considerably smaller than a

The type of water chub adore.

thumb-sized piece of bread. I used to live right on the River Wensum and from my window I could see great numbers of chub on most days lying on the gravel where the current was quite quick. After a while those fish became suspicious of large baits, but they were quite happy to take sweetcorn, for example, especially when it was fed in quite large quantities. Ledgered sweetcorn hardly ever got a bite and it had to be float fished down to them to provoke any real response. The perfect float for this was, of course, the Avon. This had the body to deal with the fairly quick water and at the same time was not pulled under. However, the water was quite shallow and very clear and I soon found that a traditional Avon quite obviously spooked the fish. The answer was to fish way overdepth and keep holding back dramatically. It was not totally successful but it did catch chub.

Interestingly, over the last year or two I have fished the same swims again, but this time the crystal Avon has been available to me. There is little doubt that this arouses far less suspicion amongst chub in the shallow, clear swims, and the chub have seemed quite happy to take corn from under the float itself. Of course, Wensum chub being what they are, they will soon wise up to the crystal Avon as they have done to everything else. Still, there is no doubt that I caught a good few fish using this float that would have been denied me by any other method. It is quite amazing how a small thing will change complete failure to at least moderate success. I used to find this when I taught boys fly fishing. Many of them would do ninety to ninety-five per cent of things correctly, and yet they would still struggle to catch anything but the most naive

of stock fish. Very frequently they had to make only one small correction before bigger, wiser trout would be theirs. The difference between success and failure was like a knife edge.

It is just the same with a species like chub in a hard-fished, clear river like the Wensum. There are times when the chub appear to be absolutely uncatchable and nothing you can do will get a bite. You really feel like tearing your hair out, and then, out of the blue, you stumble on to a tiny little trick which totally reverses the situation. The moral, I feel sure, is just to keep on trying things and to keep thinking things through. After all, we do have considerably more brain and logical power than the chub – even though they seem to have all the advantages down there in the crystal water where it really counts.

A float can frequently outscore the lead.

Very often, the water can be on the angler's side – as it was for me recently on a trip to the River Wye. The river had fined down considerably and visibility was about 18in. I found the fish in a slow, deep hole, close under my own bank, and heavy feeding brought quite big chub for the Wye up close to the surface. The float I used for this job was the wire stick. This pattern probably would have emptied the swim on the crystal-clear Wensum, but here on the coloured water the chub simply ignored it. The wire Avon is a nice, stable float which I needed as there were one or two quicker bits of current. Also, the wire stick provided a certain amount of inbuilt weight and I could get away with accordingly less shot on the line. I found that the chub were frequently taking the bait on the drop as a result, and during one afternoon I had just over twenty-five fish from a swim barely 5yd long. I suspect that I had caught virtually every fish in it, and returning them to the water immediately after capture didn't seem to harm things at all.

It was that same afternoon that I saw a very big chub indeed about 80yd downriver. I could not get close to it, however, because I was fishing on the point of a big lagoon and the way downriver was barred by both water and impenetrable bushes. I took off the wire stick, rummaged in my bag and came up with the largest loafer that carries five swan shot. Two swans acted as trapper shot and three swans as the bulk shot 2ft beneath. A couple of feet below that (I couldn't be bothered to be too precise) I tied on a size 10 hook with a good

A night float can often prove deadly for chub at close range.

sized lobworm. In fact, the lobworm was of such a good size that it sank the float – consequently, I took one of the bulk shot off. Then I simply let the float go down with the current.

Visibility was no problem and the big loafer took the river in its stride. I caught two or three smaller chub in the first five swims down and missed a bite. On the sixth swim down I got the float to around the area where the big chub had moved and it arrowed under. I stuck into something that felt very big (a lot of fish do at that range in fast water) and it was off after only ten or fifteen seconds. I wound in to find the hook gone. As I was tying on another, a large, red salmon leaped three times clear of the water! Who knows, loafer floats may be selling well on the River Tay before we know it.

BARBEL

It was the River Severn that really opened my eyes to barbel fishing. I fished it first for these fish during the late 1970s at a time when I was having considerable success in Norfolk's River Wensum for the same species. Back in Norfolk, I was using all the traditional specialist techniques and was succeeding well. On the Severn, however, I by and large failed and was given a round lesson in adaptability by Ron Lees. I realized then that there was more than one way of catching barbel and that the big, ledgered bait did not work in all circumstances.

At that period, Ron owned a tackle shop in Droitwich and the thing that first interested me was that he had a stove behind the counter

Expert barbel man Chris Yates in action.

where hemp was constantly on the boil. Also, there were stacks of pre-packed casters piled up. His shop could not have been busier and the Severn regulars simply queued up outside the door. Ron himself took me down to the river on the Wednesday afternoon and he showed me *the* method: the swim before him was fed heavily with hemp and caster, and soon large strings of bubbles appeared on the green, oily surface as barbel began to move and guzzle beneath him.

Ron's approach was that of the matchman and he inched a comparatively light stick float on fine line through the water.

The bait, as I remember, was double caster on perhaps a size 16 hook. Sure enough Ron caught barbel for me, seemingly to order. The thing that I loved was his total calm as the fish tore away into mid-stream. He would play barbel after barbel nonchalantly, rod held high, talking to me all the time and, believe it or not, even feeding the swim as he played the fish on the end of the line. If he didn't feed the fish, he fed himself by taking large chunks out of a pork pie! Of course, on that sort of tackle a barbel could take quite a while to land, and twenty or thirty minutes was not considered a particularly long battle. In fact, I seem to remember Ron spending all one match playing just two fish – neither of which he managed to land.

At first I refused to believe the evidence of my own eyes and continued to fish in the stereotyped Wensum way. I caught nothing. That is until after dark when those Severn swims would go absolutely wild for me. In fact, one take was so violent that my 8lb line actually broke at the reel! That was all well and good, but the days in midsummer could be very long and for me very boring, and so, little by little, I began to use the matchman's approach.

Of course, all that took place thirteen or so years ago and both matchman and specialist

have developed even further since then. I would never say that barbel can only be taken on the float, of course – super fish from all the UK's rivers are taken on swimfeeders and straightforward ledgers – but the float is one of the most telling ways of presenting a barbel bait. There simply are times when they will not have it presented static.

In 1986 I found myself fishing the Royalty on a bright summer's day in the company of one Christopher Yates. He had booked himself into the Parlour, lucky dog, and I was left to fend for myself on the open river. All morning I ledgered conventionally and caught nothing. I felt that I was going to catch nothing at all that day and was completely lacking in confidence. It was only later in the afternoon that the penny dropped: the barbel were in front of me and they were feeding but they were only looking at moving baits. When a friendly spectator offered to go and buy me a float, my luck began to change. A huge piece of luncheon meat was trotted through the swim on a cork-bodied Avon and I lost three fish. That was heart-breaking, but at least my rod had been bent and I realized that once again a moving bait was essential.

It is true to say that barbel are probably not the brightest of fish but that does not mean that they can be totally scorned. Where they come under pressure and have been caught, then an education really does take place. I remember one particular small fish of only 6lb taken on the Wensum. Now, the Wensum is the perfect place to spend a barbel apprenticeship because it is so shallow and so gin-clear. This particular barbel came to examine a piece of luncheon meat lying on a gravel run no less than six times over a ninety-minute period before making its mind up! And, having made its mind up, it ignored the bait and fled to another swim! If that relatively small barbel would not have a static bait, what chance would there be with its bigger brothers?

The author fishing the Avon.

The River Wye – barbel and pike water supreme.

Of course, many barbel fishermen still insist on fishing without a float and would rather freeline or fish a rolling ledger. Again, both approaches have merit but freelining does frequently cause a problem with bite indication, and a rolling ledger almost invariably begins to pull off true course and angle in towards the banks in an unnatural fashion. The float, though, can trundle a bait perfectly naturally over gravels and past feeding barbel until it slides decisively under.

When asked what the best barbel bait was, Bill Warren (the old-time Avon maestro) apparently replied: 'Elvers, then bullheads, then gudgeon.' Those words always lived with me and on at least three rivers I have found them to be true. In the earlier part of the summer small deadbaits fished on the quicker gravel runs do take very good barbel indeed. Actually, I suspect that the very biggest fish are at least half-predatorial. Of course, a bullhead can be ledgered and it does waver very enticingly in the current. It can also be freelined to makes its own way downriver, but I still don't feel that anything can beat its presentation under a suitable

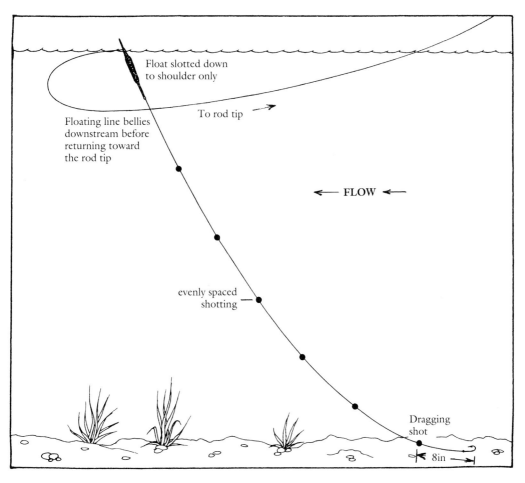

Float slotted down
to shoulder only

To rod tip →

Floating line bellies
downstream before
returning toward
the rod tip

← FLOW ←

evenly spaced
shotting —

Dragging
shot

8in

Fig. 36 Shot dragger.

loafer-type float. The loafer is buoyant enough to allow one swan shot to bump along the bottom without continually submerging. This swan slows the passage of the bait down, and with skilful mending of the line and holding back, the water can be searched very effectively. In my experience, when a barbel takes a bullhead presented in this way it is a very positive affair, and in clear water you'd think that the loafer was going to bury itself in the bottom.

Now, look at the diagram (*see* Fig. 36) of the shot dragger. The concept is an easy one:

to inch a small bait delicately and convincingly through a slow- to medium-paced barbel swim. There are days when you know that the barbel are present but they are just not having the bait – this is when the shot dragger comes into its own.

I can do no better than describe one particular day with the method to show how it works. The swim was around 8ft deep – about perfect for the method which is actually effective up to around 10–11ft. The water was moving quite slowly from left to right and there was next to no wind. I knew barbel were there – one rolled and I had two or three fish the previous day – but I just could not get a bite. They would not look at a ledgered bait and the water was too slow to freeline or to roll any sort of ledger. The shot dragger, however, allowed me to present small baits (pieces of sweetcorn) right in the spots where I suspected the fish to be and to trundle the bait right into their mouths. I was fishing about four lengths out and put in a few handfuls of sweetcorn well upstream to settle the area. The float moves extremely slowly with this method and frequently looks as though it's going to pull over as the bait lodges on the bottom or drags against a piece of debris. Sometimes it does go down altogether, and you have to flick it to get it on the move again. Bites, though, are a different thing entirely and are ridiculously positive.

On this particular day I caught six barbel. Each one simply buried the float and although I struck at many more indications, I felt I hit every true bite that I was presented with. I have little doubt in my mind that if I had continued with the quivertip and swimfeeder that day I would have been lucky to have caught a brace of fish. This method was both entertaining and effective, and I really believe that if even a sullen barbel has a bait dragged right up to its snout there is a very fair chance that it will take it if the bait is not moving too quickly and looks natural enough.

DACE

During the summer in particular, dace of all sizes are found in shallower, faster water – often beneath mill-pools and weirs. It is possible that they are there for the extra oxygen that they require for spawning, or simply because the fly hatches tend to be more abundant in such places. In fact, dace are very

much surface feeders – not exclusively by any means, but they are the trout of the coarse world in their feeding habits. As a child I used to enjoy capitalizing on this habit by fishing for them very much on the surface, and it is a method that I still enjoy. Tackle could not be simpler: a normal float rod, thick-spool reel, 2.6lb line to the hook, a very small quill float and a size 18 hook is all that is needed.

Floating casters are an essential part of the whole game and have to be trickled in at the head of a stretch where dace are rising at flies. Very soon, the dace will switch over to the casters just as happily as they fed off the natural insect. It pays to feed down the same line, about one or two rod lengths out, but do not overfeed the swim as too many casters will simply break up the dace shoal. You might even lose the shoal altogether as the individual fish move off downstream after escaping casters. Remember, feed just a steady trickle.

The method is simplicity itself. The line to the float is buoyant and there is no shot between float and hook. The trick is to present the caster in the taking lane as naturally as possible. That, of course requires that you mend the line a fair bit and hold the float back. If the float precedes the caster, then you are in trouble. It is a good idea to know exactly how far from the float your caster will be riding and to look in that general direction for a rising dace. Generally, the dace will move the float, but this is not always so. Quite frequently they will eject the caster before the float has slid from one side of the current to the other. In fact, if you are pretty certain that you have had a take, it pays to strike at once. This is another advantage of not swamping your swim with floating casters: if there are too many going down there will be so many rises that you will not be able to see one to your own hookbait.

Naturally, the floating caster has to be presented perfectly for it to succeed – as with any floating bait. If you are having any real problems inducing a bite, then try using a sinking caster on the hook. You probably find that the dace will take this with much less hesitation than they will the floating object. It is simply a more forgiving type of presentation and you should find that the float zips away quite decisively.

This method tends to work best in the evening, especially in the early summer or midsummer. Often there might be quite a natural fly hatch which is bringing the dace to the surface anyway, but, as I have said, they are unlikely to be preoccupied with the natural article.

Traditionally, anglers have always trotted the stream for dace and the method is great fun. A small stick float with number six or eight shot placed at intervals down the line, a 1.7lb test bottom to size 18 hook with a single or double caster constitutes pretty much the favourite rig. Sometimes the bites are very quick or do not even register. In this case, the 'tell-tale' shot, usually a number eight, is in the wrong position. About 18in from the hook is generally the best place to start, but move it down to about 1ft if problems continue.

Loose feeding is often quite enough to keep the dace interested, but sometimes bait mixed into groundbait, and mixed hard, can

Grayling often inhabit the fast-flowing shallows along with the dace.

pull them down to the bottom, whereby it's generally easier to hit. Feed can be overdone, however, for dace are not large and their appetites are limited. Six, seven or eight maggots per swim downriver is the average on most rivers. However, it is advisable to increase this amount substantially if you are fishing larger scale rivers like the Wye where the shoals can be absolutely massive. It is also tempting to throw in a handful of maggots before the start, but this has in the past killed the swim stone dead. Little and often is the best way with dace I feel sure, gradually building up the swim to a climax.

Both of these methods can be great dace catchers on their day but not necessarily for the biggest fish. In fact, it has been my experience over the years that the big dace often tend to behave rather like roach. They will inhabit deeper, slower stretches of the river, especially from autumn onwards. They move in shoals but often very small ones and quite frequently share the same area with roach. In my experience, very frequently the float has gone under and a small roach has turned out to be a big dace.

All the usual roach fishing methods will work with these super dace that are often well over 10oz in weight. For bait, you cannot beat a pinch of flake on a size 12 or even a size 10 hook, and bites are extremely confident most of the time.

You can lay on, stret peg or even inch a float slowly along a crease – it does not really seem to matter, providing the piece of flake is working close to the bottom in as natural a way as possible. I am sure that the next record dace will be caught in much this sort of fashion and in fact, as I write, I have already heard of a 1lb 6oz dace that has fallen to a roach fisherman in a back-end deep hole.

Do remember, however, that feeding once again has to be light. Even a 12oz dace is not a truly big fish and can easily be overfed. Half a slice of mashed bread makes a good start and a further quarter of a slice can be fed in every third or fourth cast. Try to keep the baiting and the casting as accurate as possible with these small amounts because the bread can swirl around the pool and easily be lost, doing little or no good.

There is no doubt that the very biggest dace are caught at dusk or even during the first couple of hours into darkness. This is where a Betalight float really comes into its own. With the Betalight you can see bites – even finicky ones – just as well as you can in broad daylight and you can extend your float fishing sessions way into the best time of all for a real specimen.

Bibliography

Over the decades there have been many excellent books published on float fishing. Sadly most of them are now out of print and unobtainable. The following books offer a large amount of information and are still readily available:

The Complete Book of Coarse Fishing (Collins-Willow, 1992).
Carp, Quest for the Queen (2nd edn), John Bailey and Martyn Page (Crowood, 1990).
The Complete Book of Float Fishing, Allan Haines (David & Charles, 1989).
Roach: The Gentle Giants, John Bailey (Crowood, 1987).

For those wishing to perfect their float fishing techniques, the popular monthly magazine *Improve Your Coarse Fishing* is well worth investing in on a regular basis.

Index

INDEX